Bullets That
Changed America

Bullets That Changed America

Thirteen Historic Assassinations, Duels, Misfires and Murders

PETER ZABLOCKI

McFarland & Company, Inc., Publishers
Jefferson, North Carolina

ISBN (print) 978-1-4766-8946-3
ISBN (ebook) 978-1-4766-4732-6

LIBRARY OF CONGRESS AND BRITISH LIBRARY
CATALOGUING DATA ARE AVAILABLE

Library of Congress Control Number 2022025951

Police officer firing his gun in a demonstration
of a bulletproof vest in 1923 (Library of Congress)

Printed in the United States of America

*McFarland & Company, Inc., Publishers
Box 611, Jefferson, North Carolina 28640
www.mcfarlandpub.com*

For Deidra

Acknowledgments

This book would not be possible without the patience, encouragement, and support from my wife and two amazing children who were there every step of the way. I would also like to thank those who provided some food for thought as I was figuring out the stories embedded in these pages, especially Dr. Steve Racine, Vito Bianco, Matthew Arroyo, and Heather Pollak. I would also like to thank the teachers who encouraged me—either as educators or colleagues—to look at history in a different way; specifically James Saganiec, Dr. Theodore F. Cook, George C. Robb, Kevin Kane, Matthew Higgins, Scott Gamable, Danielle Elia, and countless others. A special mention also goes to Ms. Laura Petersen, Siobhan Koch, Maryellen Liddy, Joyce Peslak, and all the other librarians who have helped me with acquiring the proper resources I needed over the years. Last but not least, thank you to J. Banks Smither and Michael Dolan for being the first ones to give me a chance to write professionally—I will forever be in your debt.

Table of Contents

Preface

One does not need to be a historian or history teacher to have heard about the assassinations of John F. Kennedy, Abraham Lincoln, or Martin Luther King. But let us say that you are an amateur historian or that you were that one student that never missed a single moment in your high school history class—or you are still sitting in your high school history class. If that is the case, you might even throw Presidents William McKinley and James Garfield or Alexander Hamilton into the mix of famous people in American history who met their end through a speeding bullet. And that is assuming that we all heard about the "shot heard around the world"—pun intended. I have taught history to American teenagers for nearly two decades, and one thing has become clear: they are fascinated with historical crime, intrigue, and violence. And I do not mean that they want to perpetuate violent acts themselves. No. Teens—and adults, for that matter—love stories of wars, battles, duels, and assassinations. And while a good Netflix show or a cozy mystery novel garners a certain level of people's attention, nothing seems to draw us in more than events that happened in real life.

Sometimes we forget that history has the word "story" right in it. When examining past events, even those that are not always pleasant, we realize that the only constant in the study of the past is change. As ironic as it may seem, the past is indeed full of change. As if a dance between causes and effects—whereas in some cases, one event can be both a cause and a product—small actions often have consequences that reverberate for many years. Sometimes something as small as a bullet fired by a single individual could be resounding enough to move a nation. And while often the person pulling the trigger is lost to history—John Wilkes Booth or Lee Harvey Oswald excluded—the victim is not. Most of us have heard of some of the more infamous assassinations and how they shaped our nation's history. For example, how the assassination of JFK resulted in the ascendance of Lyndon B. Johnson to the presidency and his subsequent escalation of the war in Vietnam. Or the assassination of Martin Luther King, Jr., and the ultimate crumbling of the continued civil rights movement. Or even the what-ifs of history that are often spoken of when discussing the assassination of Robert F. Kennedy, or President McKinley, whose death opened the door to a Teddy Roosevelt presidency. Yet, history is also full of lesser-known actions that have equally echoing outcomes. Some were small individual mistakes or misjudgments that altered the course of already known events. Others were small actions of violence that sparked the affairs now highlighted throughout our history textbooks.

In these pages, you will learn how a young George Washington found himself in an armed conflict against the French and Native Americans in 1754. In those days, the man who would be called the "Father of His Country" kept himself warm with a British redcoat. You will travel with the Native American leader Tecumseh on his failed yet noble quest to unite the eastern tribes into an all-out resistance to push the settlers out of their lands once and for all. And you will see the violent beginnings of a national division that would soon turn into the bloodiest conflict in all of the nation's history. You will also examine a turning point within the Civil War that is not often discussed yet interestingly crucial to its outcome. The stories found here frequently showcase the rebellious spirit of the American people—their impulse to resist, to fight for their beliefs—and the power struggle between those who possess it and those who oppose it. The struggle between Native Americans of the Great Plains and a nation on the move. The struggles of the working class for significance in a newly industrialized economy. The tension between anarchy, communism, and democratic rule in a nation afraid of change. And the eternal struggle for equality of the races. There are stories of men who sacrificed their lives for their nation only to see that nation turn against them—seen in the story of the World War I veterans' Bonus March or the more recent societal rejection of Vietnam War veterans.

I attempted, where possible, to tell the story of each moment and each specific bullet fired from the perspective of the people who were there to witness it—sometimes even doing the firing or being felled by the fateful shot. A "boots on the ground" approach of sorts. Each story begins with a first point-of-view retelling of the event and is then placed in historical context and further examined for its significance. These are stories as much about regular people forgotten by history as they are about the events that define who we are as a nation. After all, one might not automatically think of Richard Mentor or Black Coyote when thinking of some of the most significant turning points in Native American history. Nor would William Hushka or Paul Meadlo spring to mind as two of the most important war veterans in the annals of American history. How about Jimmie Lee Jackson, the man responsible for one of the most monumental pieces of civil rights legislation? You are unlikely to have heard about these people, for they are not typically included in the pantheon of history. They are not the Washingtons, the Jeffersons, the Kings, or the Roosevelts. They are just regular people. And for the first time collectively, their stories are combined to frame a narrative of United States history, joined by different single bullets. Bullets that resulted in paradigm shifts, making the men who fired them or died from them an alternative and perhaps truer pantheons of American history.

The work that you hold in your hands intends to supplement the existing research into the most critical events in the history of the United States. It does not intend to be an all-encompassing history but a way to highlight the causes and effects of some of the lesser-known yet equally important events in it. The impetus for each of the stories is a single bullet. Sometimes we know who fired it, but sometimes we do not. We know the bullets' final destinations and, more importantly, the repercussions they caused for the nation's course. It is truly enlightening to trace to single acts of violence so many events that we today see as monumental to the growth of our country and its people. If there is a hidden message, meaning, causation, or correlation behind that notion, it is without intent. This is not a book about American violence but perhaps more of a book about selected acts of violence in America. It does not set out to assign blame to any one person or group but to highlight the transcendent power that one brief moment or one often uncalculated decision or a reflex could have on the trajectory of a country's history. At its core, this is a story of single moments that moved a nation through unconventional causes and effects.

1

An Unfortunate Encounter,
May 28, 1754

A bullet was sailing towards the French ensign, Joseph Coulon de Villiers de Jumonville. He could not know that his fate on that day would be much worse than any harm that could come from a single bullet. Within minutes, the representative of the French government—still alive—would be tomahawked and scalped, after which Half-King—the leader of Britain's Indian allies—would scoop out the Frenchman's still warm brain and squeeze it in his hands.[1] The small skirmish between the French and the British colonist militia took all but 15 minutes and left 10 dead and more wounded. More importantly, it set into motion events that would go on to span multiple continents and take—according to some estimates—1,400,000 lives. But the young man who fired the first shot and ordered his men to follow did not yet know any of this. The 22-year-old George Washington had much to learn.

* * * * * *

By the turn of the eighteenth century, France and Britain were the two leading contenders for global power. The clash of the two European states had spread to their colonies, sparking conflicts in North America, India, and Africa. Soon, their attention turned to America's rich Ohio River Valley. A more remarkable dichotomy could not have existed between the powers in the New World. While the French colonists' intentions fell mainly on fur trading and converting the Native Americans to Catholicism, the British desire for permanent settlement and the cultivation of Native American lands led to many clashes with the tribal nations. In turn, by 1750, the French empire in North America—primarily based in today's Canada—had cultivated much friendlier relations—extending even to military alliances—with the Indians. In short, while the French possessed more significant territory on the continent and were friendlier with the Native Americans, the British had a greater population and continually encroached on the Native Americans' lands. As the two European powers began expanding into the Ohio River Valley, they were on a collision course that would spark the greater French and Indian War and eventually evolve into the more global Seven Years' War.

The French spent a considerable amount of time forging relationships with Native Americans who in turn allowed them to expand their trapping and trading empire further south into Ohio. To safeguard their interests, the European power began constructing a chain of forts southward from Lake Erie. This culminated in 1754 with the construction of Fort Duquesne at the joining point of the Allegheny and Monongahela rivers. Today, the area would be more in line with the location of modern Pittsburgh, but in the eighteenth century, it was the heartland of the Ohio River Valley. Unfortunately, at least for the English, the French built their fort on land previously marked off as belonging to the British Crown and approved for cultivation by wealthy Virginia planters. Alarmed by what he was hearing, Virginia Governor Robert Dinwiddie petitioned King George II of England for permission to meet the threat head-on in 1753, a full year before the completion of the latest fort. In possession of a blunt but somewhat courteous letter from the British governor to the French colonial government, a 21-year-old inexperienced major of the Virginia militia set off to warn the French to vacate the territory. It was October 1753, and George Washington was still six months away from the biggest blunder of his young career.

On his first journey out west on behalf of the British Crown, the young soldier battled many circumstances that might have foreshadowed his eventual bad luck in dealing with the French. The young party traveled on foot, by canoe, and on horseback through the perilous wilderness. Perhaps poignantly, Washington's arrival at Fort Le Boeuf, near Lake Erie, while met with courteousness, produced a sharp rebuff from the French leadership. Examining the fortifications, George made specific sketches of the fort and surrounding grounds and quickly set off back to Virginia with the bad news. Fighting unruly weather and frequent snowstorms, the young major was nearly drowned and mutilated by frostbite. At one point, a Native American even shot at him from nearly point-blank range, missing by mere inches. Washington chose to travel through the night and build a raft to cross the frosty Allegheny to throw him off their track.

1. An Unfortunate Encounter, May 28, 1754

It was here that the major was knocked off the makeshift boat and nearly drowned or froze to death. The report of his journey, commissioned by Dinwiddie and sent over to England shortly after George's return, quickly made the relatively unknown Virginian the talk of the colony.

When news arrived in the spring of 1754 of the nearly complete construction of Fort Duquesne at the Forks of the Ohio, the governor once again sent the now newly promoted Lieutenant Colonel George Washington out west. This time his mission was to support another company commanded by William Trent, which was already marching towards the important position where the Allegheny and Mononga-hela rivers join to form the Ohio River. The men were to assist in constructing a British fort to counter the one under construction by the French. By the time his company of 159 men reached the area, the British fort was already in French possession, with the opposing side taking it without having to fire a single shot. Having been informed that a British force had surrendered to a larger French one and that the governor was ordering additional companies to the area, Washington incorrectly assumed he was now at the point of a larger delegation of soldiers. The eager young lieutenant continued his advance. Yet, instead of seeing other units catching up, Washington found himself and his force deep within enemy territory. At this point, the French and British governments were not at war but simply amidst a regional dispute.

Washington's forces made camp in Great Meadows on May 24 and awaited further orders. As they prepared to erect a small fort, scouts and traders in retreat from French soldiers stopped to report that French parties were active in his area.[2] A panicky Washington did not want to become the subject of yet another dishonorable surrender. He knew that, if discovered, his location would surely point to the fact that he was commanding but a small force. Washington needed to cut the French off before they reached his position, forcing him to surrender. It was also around this time that he received orders from Dinwiddie allowing him to not only restrain any French intruders, but "kill and destroy" them if necessary.[3] Camped nearby Washington's strategic location was a Native American who had scouted with him the last time the young man ventured into the Ohio River Valley. Known to his men as Tanacharison, the Native American was more commonly referred to by the British as Half-King. George was aware of the presence of his former scout's camp and was not alarmed when Half-King showed up near his fire on May 27, warning him of a nearby French encampment. Having made up his mind, the lieutenant colonel accepted the Native American's assistance in leading him and a smaller detached force of 40 men to his date with destiny.

* * * * * *

It is safe to say that while trailing Half-King and his men in single file through heavy underbrush, Washington was aware the French and the British were not at war and that his orders were defensive. Still, he made up his mind that the French unit he was approaching was surely there to attack him. "That very moment, I ... ordered my ammunition to be put in a place of safety ... left a guard to defend it, and with the rest of my men, [continued] in heavy rain," he recalled years later. "And in a night as dark as pitch, along a patch scarce broad enough for one man; we were sometimes fifteen or twenty minutes out of the Path, before we could come to it again, and so dark, that we would often strike one against another."[4] Traveling all through the night, and with dawn upon them, Washington's forces finally emerged from the wilderness onto a glen's rim above the secluded French soldiers in a murky hollow below. The morning fires had not yet reached their full blaze. Washington chose to organize his attack from the top of the ridge as the Native Americans in his company sneaked down below to flank the French and prevent any of them from escaping. "We were advanced pretty near them, as we thought, when they discovered us; whereupon I ordered my Company to fire."[5]

According to a firsthand account discovered by historian David Preston in 2018, the young colonel fired the first shot. "Col. Washington begun himself and fired and then his people," wrote one of Half-King's warriors some years later.[6] The same man contended that the French traded volleys with the English, "two or three Fires of as many Pieces as would go off, being rainy Weather." The French, "having taken to their Heels and running, happening to run the Way the Half King was with his Warriors, eight of them met with their Destiny by the Indian Tomayhawks."[7] The 21 remaining men huddled near the British forces that had descended from the ridge. According to historical accounts, their cries for mercy against the Indian tomahawks added to the pervasive melancholy. Apart from one Frenchman who managed to slip away into the woods and eventually notify other French military units of what had transpired, nine French soldiers were killed and then promptly toma-hawked and scalped.

Lying near a tree was a still alive French ensign, Joseph Coulon de Villiers de Jumonville. Using hand gestures and his native French tongue, which Washington and his men did not understand, the man attempted to explain to the young lieutenant colonel that he was a diplomat who was simply delivering a letter to the British imploring them to leave the French lines. To his dismay, nobody seemed to understand what he was saying. Although disputed for generations, it is widely believed that Washington was startled when Half-King, standing behind him, finally spoke French. The warrior pushed the younger colonel aside and moved swiftly towards the wounded man with the rain beating down upon him. "Tu n'es pas encore mort, mon pere!" (Thou art not yet dead, my father) said the Native American as his tomahawk came down upon the ensign's head.[8] Moving the tool around, Half-King cracked the Frenchman's skull open and proceeded to grasp his brain. Some accounts go so far as claiming that he even consumed some of it.

A young Frenchman who witnessed the event from the woods where he had gone to relieve himself shortly before the attack commenced now ran barefoot as fast as he could. The next day, the commanding officer at Fort Duquesne stumbled and sat down in his seat upon hearing of the news from the exhausted soldier standing before him.

A young George Washington was still wearing a red coat on his back when he defended the Crown in the French and Indian War, which he might have played a small part in instigating (Library of Congress).

Bullets That Changed America

George Washington and his men began a withdrawal 10 miles back to their original camp, constructing a rickety stockade fittingly named Fort Necessity. Meanwhile, initially in Canada but soon in France, men seethed with rage over the murder of their peaceful envoy by the treacherous British. The dead man's brother, the Sieur Coulon de Villiers, came marching hotly from Montréal to avenge the assassin—his 900 men would clash with Washington's on July 3.[9]

In the end, George Washington's forces were too weak to defend either the forks of the Ohio as a whole or his little fort. He ironically surrendered himself and his troops on July 4—a date that would have a much different meaning for the man in his future. Equally ironic is that the French were generous enough to let him and his men march out of Ohio alive. They did this after misinterpreting his confession of being involved in the death of de Jumonville as admittance to having murdered him himself, and thus admitting his mistake and apologizing. Apart from having Washington capitulate and admit to his crime, there was not much else the French army could do without further adding to the already tense relations between the two nations. Thus, they let the now starved and outnumbered men simply retreat. After all, France was not at war with Britain. But that was just a matter of time.

* * * * * *

In the eyes of his peers, the bullet—or musket ball—Washington fired on May 28, 1754, all but stopped his ascendance into colonial prominence as well as his climb up the British military ranks. Yet, looking at it long-term, the event's significance was bigger than the colonel's reputation. It took another 19 months for the two empires to officially declare what came to be known as the Seven Years' War. But that did not mean that the nations' colonists did not continue the fight Washington started. The French and Indian War, which would set in motion the more significant conflict for American independence in 20 years, had begun.

The blame for potentially starting a war poured in on Washington from all sides. First, it came from the Crown, then his detractors in the colonies, and then, of course, from the French. He was not allowed to fret for too long; within months of the defeat at Fort Necessity, the young man was once again sent back to the Ohio River Valley as an aide to the British general Edward Braddock. Their mission was to drive out the French once and for all. The French mother country pulled out all the stops to protect their interests in the New World. Eighteen ships carrying six battalions or regulars—3,000 men in all—sailed from France to America.[10] Braddock did not have to worry too much about the ships, as the British learned of the voyage and sent their navy to intercept. Ultimately only two ships made it through to the colonies.

The French and their Native American allies repelled the British general's attack on Fort Duquesne with nearly 1,500 British soldiers. Accustomed to the British style of marching in rows towards the battle, Braddock and his troops were no match for the guerrilla tactics that awaited them. Not only did the general commit his soldiers to slaughter and a major defeat, but he also met his end at the battle for the forks of the Ohio. While the British regulars were once again embarrassed by the French, the Virginia militia commanded by George Washington fared much better. "I luckily escaped without a wound, though I had four bullets through my coat and two horses shot under me," recalled the lieutenant colonel.[11] Having safely returned his regiment home, the future president of the United States saw his reputation greatly improve. He was swiftly promoted and put in charge of all Virginian troops. He was only 23 years old.

The first two years of the war, which began with Washington's skirmish in 1754, went terribly for the British in the Americas. After Braddock's defeat, the entire frontier was open to merciless French and Indian attacks. Confusion ruled back in England as the British Crown formally declared war on France, officially marking the beginning of the Seven Years' War. The much-needed change came in 1757 as King George II, angered by French victories, selected William Pitt as the new leader of colonial policy in America. Under Pitt's direction, the British finally began to win some battles. The most significant was the Battle of Québec, which became the final English victory in the continental conflict. Pitt's most important change in policy was recruiting new Native American allies—namely the Iroquois—to counterbalance the French superiority gained through their Native American collaborators. Newly appointed generals Jeffery Amherst and James Wolfe finally secured Fort Duquesne, renamed it Fort Pitt, and conquered Québec.

By 1759, using the night for cover, Wolfe's armies scaled the protective cliffs surrounding Québec, the stronghold of New France. When the French commander, the marquis of Montcalm, woke up to redcoats storming his stronghold, it was too late for him to stop the inevitable. Historian David Muzzey wrote in his *A History of Our County* in 1936: "The fall of Quebec was the decisive event of the French and Indian War. Amherst entered Montreal with little opposition the next year, and the English fleets completed the downfall of France and her ally Spain by seizing the rich sugar islands of Guadeloupe and Martinique in the West Indies and by capturing Havana in Cuba and Manila in the Philippines."[12] The fall of Québec hastily led to the official end of the conflict known the world over as the Seven Years' War, or more commonly referred to in United States textbooks as the French and Indian War. Britain claimed all of North America east of the Mississippi River and granted Spain all of the land west of the mighty river, including New Orleans. All that remained of France's New World holdings were the West Indies and a few small islands near Newfoundland.

Speaking after the British victory, French minister Choiseul correctly predicted that the colonies would "shake off their dependence" on England sooner rather than later. With the French menace gone from their borders, he reasoned, it would be impossible to keep the American colonists in due submission.[13] Two years after the 1763 Treaty of Paris ended the global conflict, the colonists were indeed at odds with England over taxation. By the end of another decade, they would be at war with their mother country. Shortly thereafter, they would become a sovereign nation.

With the French gone from the Ohio River Valley, an Ottawa leader named Pontiac realized that nothing stopped the British colonists from encroaching on Native American lands. By the spring of 1763, the chief, backed by a united force of various Ohio tribes, managed to capture nearly 10 British forts. Having barely succeeded in quieting the uprising—and only after spreading smallpox through disease-infested blankets—the British Crown set off to avoid further conflicts with Native Americans. The reality was that they could not afford to have another war, having just fought against France for world dominance. Consequently, the British issued the Proclamation of 1763, which prohibited any colonial expansion into lands past the Appalachian Mountains. The colonists, however, would not be deterred. Seeing the proclamation as a means of halting their expansion, the colonists were convinced that the king was working against their freedoms. The second result of the French and Indian War, the British war debt, only further compounded this feeling. Having found itself in a financial crisis following the war, Britain instituted more zealous policies towards their American colonies. The consequences of these changes could not have gone any worse for England.

Once the dust settled at the end of 1763, Britain found itself ruling over a territory double the size of its 13 original colonies in the Americas. Concurrently, the new land acquired was home to more than 200,000 Indians, "many of them ready to believe the stories which the French soldiers and traders spread among them, that their new masters the English were planning to rob them of their hunting fields."[14] To protect their interests, and following Pontiac's Rebellion, the British settled on 10,000 as appropriate for the number of troops required in the New World. The Crown added this cost to the national debt, which had already doubled during the war. In fact, because of the war, which started with Washington's skirmish in the Ohio River Valley, taxes in England had risen to four shillings in every pound or 20 per cent.[15] Ironically, the colonists did not initially see their taxes raised. Many in England questioned why their cousins across the pond did not contribute to the burden of paying for their protection, first from the French, and now the Native Americans. The British government, facing an angry uprising back home, saw no other way but to implement the idea of taxing the American colonies—with tragic results.

* * * * * *

And thus, after having spent the whole rainy night climbing through dense forests in single file, the 22-year-old lieutenant colonel, tired and cold from the march, could not foresee the fate that awaited him. He also could not predict how his eagerness would lead to creating a new nation two decades later—one that would cement itself as the most powerful nation in the world by the mid–twentieth century. By then, his name and birthday would be celebrated with mattress and car sales. Standing on that ledge, George Washington did not yet know any of that. He steadied himself. Put his finger on the trigger and pulled. And so began the history of the United States.

For Further Reading

There are many books written about George Washington's life and military career. Yet, a great start would have to be the Pulitzer

Prize-winning *Washington: A Life* by Ron Chernow (2011)—specifically "Part One: The Frontiersman." For a more detailed account of the event itself, one could turn to the more recent *The Indian World of George Washington: The First President, the First Americans, and the Birth of the Nation* (2019) by Colin Calloway—a National Book Award finalist. One could, of course, turn to the study of the great conflict itself. In that case, an excellent survey of the topic (and one tackled easily) would be Walter R. Borneman's *The French and Indian War: Deciding the Fate of North America* (2001). Or there is the even shorter *The War That Made America: A Short History of the French and Indian War* (2006) by Fred Anderson, eventually turned into a PBS documentary. For a more detailed account of the story told in this chapter, I would turn to the nearly 1000-page *The Crucible of War: The Seven Years' War and the Fate of Empire in British North America, 1754–1776* (2000), also by Fred Anderson. Chapters 3 through 6 would be especially of interest to those wanting to analyze and evaluate the role of George Washington in starting the conflict that would become the French and Indian War.

2

"Back to Your Mark, Sir!"
May 30, 1806

The two parties arrived at Harrison's Mill, the agreed-upon location on the Red River in Logan, Kentucky, in much different spirits. The parties remained separate as members of each forded the river and then regrouped at the green patch of grass near the forests that made up the Tennessee border. One party was full of laughter, the other—made up of older men—more somber and stoic. Two men, one from each party, broke away and carried out the business of measuring out 24 feet—eight paces. As the others watched, the two men tossed a large silver coin, spoke briefly in hushed voices, and seemed to have concluded the grim preparations.

Then two different men—one from each side—took positions at either end of the measured and marked distance. They stood with their pistols pointed downward. "Are you ready?" called General Thomas Overton, one of the original pair who prepped the scene. "I am ready," the younger of the two duelists answered promptly. "I am ready," echoed the other man—clearly the older of the two. "Watch that third button. It's over his heart. I shall hit him there," exclaimed Charles Dickinson, the young and eager adversary. "Fire!" yelled Overton.[1]

The bullet pierced Andrew Jackson's chest. He jerked his arm up to his left breast, where the bullet lodged itself mere millimeters from his heart. Shock on his face, Dickinson turned to his second and exclaimed, "Great God! Have I missed him?" As he stepped off of his peg in disbelief, Jackson's second, General Overton, ran up to the shocked young Tennessee marksman who never missed his target. "Back to your mark, sir!" he shouted.[2]

The man destined to one day become the president of the United States steadied himself. With the blood pooling in the hand over his heart, he raised his gun arm, once more cocked his clearly misfired weapon, and fired. The one-time U.S. representative from Tennessee, a judge of the Tennessee Supreme Court, and major general of the Tennessee militia would not die that day. He collapsed from his wounds; the bullet would stay lodged in his chest for the remainder of his life. Andrew Jackson did not yet know that one day he would be responsible for ushering in a national democratic fervor that would eventually bear his name—Jacksonian democracy—and alter the nation's social and political canvas, albeit not for all. The world will never know how different the United States would have been had Dickinson's bullet met its mark.

* * * * * *

When Andrew Jackson stepped on his mark, 24 feet away from his opponent, the United States of 1806 was a far cry from what it would become when he swore his oath of office on March 4, 1829. And the difference would be even starker by the time he stepped down from the presidency in 1836. It would be ignorant to say that the changes are all attributable to one man. Still, it would be equally flawed to ignore Andrew Jackson as a major factor in developing a new democracy that would redefine the American nation in the nineteenth century. Had Jackson fallen that summer day on the Kentucky-Tennessee border, the country—its political, social, economic, and even geographical makeup, as well as the executive office that we know today—would undoubtedly look different, for better or for worse.

The years following the duel and the beginning of Jackson's presidency marked a new turn in the development of American politics. According to historian Richard Hofstadter, the changes were all-encompassing. The two-party system disappeared, opening the door to personal, local, and sectional conflicts replacing broad differences over public policy and defining national politics. "As the presidency declined from its heights under the leadership of Washington and Jefferson, the contest for the presidential seat resolved into a scramble of local and sectional princelings for the position of heir apparent," summarized the historian.[3] The Virginia dynasty seemed to have a pattern of elevating its most prominent members of society into the highest national office, and presidential nominations could not be more remote from the popular will, as they were in the hands of the party caucuses in Congress, itself with no significant turnover in office-holders.

Apart from the political stagnation, the United States found itself amidst its first real financial panic. The Panic of 1819 set various classes of people against one another for the first time since the presidency of Thomas Jefferson. The issue stemmed from the War of 1812, which would also give Andrew Jackson his claim to fame. After the U.S. and Great Britain had fought to a draw, a wave of nationalism swept the nation. With the charter of Hamilton's first national bank expired, the U.S. found itself fighting a war with neither uniform currency nor the ability to raise funds. Accordingly, a second national bank was chartered only to become the focus of public resentment.

As emphasized by historian Eric Foner, the Second Bank of the United States was a private, profit-making corporation that served as the government's financial agent, issuing paper money, collecting taxes, and paying the government's debts.[4] It was also tasked with ensuring that any paper money issued by local banks had real value. Yet instead of proper regulation, the national bank gave local banks free rein in extending loans for land—especially in the West and South—to those hyped by the post-war overseas market demand for American cotton and grain. The inflated demand for loans and concurrent printing of money past the gold and silver standard came to a screeching halt in early 1819 when Europe's demand fell and the speculative bubble burst. Hofstadter said it best when describing what followed: "The banks, which had grossly overextended themselves, were forced to press their debtors to the wall, and through the process of foreclosure, the national bank practically became a great absentee owner of Western and Southern property."[5] Many Americans, specifically from the West and the South, felt that they could no longer trust their banks or the politicians who supported them.

Concurrent with Jackson's rise among the Tennessee social class—first as a wealthy planter, lawyer, and slaveholder, later as statesmen and justice of the Supreme Court, and eventually a general, national hero, and the president of the United States—was a change in the nation's very own character. Historians, specifically Frederick Turner, have claimed that the frontier has, with its continual march westward, had one of the most significant influences on American history—and in this case it most certainly did. As the West was finally opened for settlement after the War of 1812, with the real and the perceived threat of Native American and British aggression in the region under control, emigrants flooded past the Allegheny Mountains. This frontier became home to a different type of settler. The westerners, in their struggle against nature and Native Americans, became self-reliant, resourceful, and courageous.[6] As the region did not beckon the wealthy easterners, this new breed of men developed a different sense of democracy. Each person was as good as any other, politically and socially.

Five new states were added to the Union in six years: Indiana (1816), Mississippi (1817), Illinois (1818), Alabama (1819), and Missouri (1821). By the census of 1820, more than a quarter of the U.S. population (2,600,000 out of 9,600,000) dwelt in the trans-Allegheny states, which sent 16 of the 46 senators and 47 of the 213 representatives to Congress.[7] For the first time, the voice of a western pioneer was equal to that of any aristocratic planter in the South or merchant in the North. What becomes important in studying the rise of and the subsequent age of Jackson is that all the states that entered the Union during this time did so with constitutions that provided for universal white suffrage (men only, of course) regardless of land ownership. Consequently, four additional original states had altered their constitutions to do the same. This extension of suffrage gave a political voice and influence to poor farmers and the new working class of the eastern states, which adopted similar changes. The labor class of recent immigrants toiling in New York and Pennsylvania factories without much independence would eventually become the final piece needed for Jackson's presidential victory in 1828.

Hofstadter would write that these poor farmers and workers, generally subordinated in the political corporations and remote from the choicest spoils of the Northern and Southern aristocracies, believed in the common feeling that popular will should control the choice of public officers and formation of public policy.[8] The result of market expansion that followed the War of 1812 and the subsequent land speculation and irresponsible banking practices that all together caused the Panic of 1819 impacted the whole nation, but nowhere more so than in the West and the Deep South. When the turn came for these now politically aware voters—the so-called common men—to choose a candidate for president in 1824, only one man fit the bill. In a sense, the changing face of America needed a representative, one who would take Thomas Jefferson's ideas of American Democracy dependent on a class of free and self-reliant commoners—or in his case, farmers—and use them to counter the powerful sectionalist and aristocratic urges. It was time to wrestle American democracy from the clutches of those who had been holding on to it for the benefit of themselves and their constituents—the Northern bankers and merchants and the Southern planters—and finally give it to the common man.

General Andrew Jackson happened to be the right man at the right time. The man who would come to define this new paradigm shift in American politics and society and who would take it from thought to reality—all while redefining the office of the presidency—extended his local fame into the national spotlight only after the events of May 30, 1806. It is safe to say that the qualities that drew him to his constituents and vice versa stemmed from events that would never have taken place had Dickinson's bullet pierced his chest just a little bit lower.

* * * * * *

Eighteen years prior to the infamous duel between the future president and Charles Dickinson, a skinny, redheaded, 20-year-old Andrew Jackson arrived in Tennessee from North Carolina with a certificate to practice law in his pocket. During the nearly two decades that followed, he cemented his reputation as a noble gentleman, frontiersman, and self-made man. Before the debacle that would find him facing a much younger man's gun at 24 feet, Jackson was already a well-respected Tennessee lawyer, fighting district attorney, congressman, senator, and state Supreme Court judge—not to mention businessman, sportsman, and husband.[9] It was the last one about which Jackson was the most sensitive.

It was no big secret that Rachel Donelson Robards married Andrew without ensuring that a divorce from her first husband, Lewis Robards, was fully finalized. The scandal came to a head when the first husband sued for divorce sometime later. And although matters were settled quickly, the gripes about Jackson being a wife-stealer and Rachel a no-lady continued for all their remaining years. According to some accounts, it was through insults directed at his wife that Jackson first came to hear of and know a young Dickinson, reputedly "the best shot in Tennessee."[10] One unverified report (which, knowing the ultimate fate of these two men, seems unlikely) has Dickinson remarking, "Gen. Jackson's wife is faster than his horses."[11] And although some of

Jackson's biographers confirm the same, as well as the fact that the general warned off Dickinson's father-in-law to control the young man, not much else came out of the exchange. Still, if true, and considering the events of May 1806, Jackson would have for sure been pointing his gun at Dickinson sooner. As it stands, it was the horse betting that would draw the two men into a lonely Kentucky field.

Dickinson, his father-in-law Captain Joseph Erwin, and Jackson, by now a general in the Tennessee militia, arranged a horse race in the fall of 1805. Erwin's horse Plow Boy did not seem ready for the clash with Jackson's famous Truxton, and the man paid the general $800 forfeit, a previously agreed-upon sum. This did not stop the townsfolk from spreading rumors that the paid sum was not right and that Erwin cheated the famous statesman. In defense of his father-in-law, Dickinson met with Jackson and, considering the matter settled, went public with his comments of blaming Jackson's supporters for stirring the pot and trying to insult his father. Additional insults and meddling from Erwin, Dickinson, and their associates—most prominently, one Thomas Swann—went back and forth, with letters appearing in local papers defending their honor and slighting Jackson's for raising suspicions and not attempting to put down the rumors. Things boiled over when Dickinson, in response to a private letter from Jackson in which the general called the young man a "base poltroon and cowardly tale-bearer ... a drunken blackguard," published a piece in the local paper calling the general "a coward."[12] Jackson had had enough. On May 22, Jackson sent his friend General Thomas Overton to the young Charles Dickinson with a proper challenge of a duel. Dr. Hanson Catlett brought a prompt reply. The request was to be granted.

The two seconds, Overton and Catlett, met on May 24 and settled on the particulars. The duel would take place on May 30 at Harrison's Mill Landing on the Red River, in Logan County, Kentucky, at 7 a.m. It would be fought at 24 feet, with the two men facing each other with pistols pointed downward; when the word "fire" was given, either could fire as soon as he pleased. On the morning of May 29, the 25-year-old Dickinson accidentally woke his wife up when getting ready, informing her that he had some business to take care of in Kentucky but that he would be back that night. In high spirits, together with his joyful and over-confident party, the young man mounted his horse and set off towards his destiny.

THE DUEL.

While no image exists of the infamous duel between Andrew Jackson and Charles Dickinson, the 1834 image used to discredit the president showcases the encounter that would forever make Jackson a "murderer" in the eyes of his political opponents (Library of Congress).

When the two parties arrived at the field that fateful morning, Jackson was wearing an oversized black coat, which perfectly hid his slender figure. According to historians, this was done at the suggestion of Overton, who masterminded the strategy to give the older man advantage over the younger sharpshooter. Historian Alfred Henry Lewis best explained the significance when he described the coat years later. "A black coat—high of collar, long of skirt," he wrote. "It buttons close to the chin; not the least glimpse of bullet guiding white of shirt collar or cravat is allowed to show.... General's lean form, tucked away in its folds, is a question not readily replied to. The only mark on the whole sable exposure of that coat is a row of steel-bright buttons that are not in the middle but peculiarly to one side."[13]

Everything went as planned that morning, and, soon enough, the two men stood facing each other at the marked-off stakes of barked pawpaw bushes. "Fire!" Dickinson's face could not hide its shock when Jackson's lanky figure remained standing. All saw his bullet hit the general. After being reprimanded for leaving his mark in disbelief, the young Dickinson looked away as he waited for Jackson's shot. Andrew Jackson raised his gun hand, took aim, and pulled the trigger. Nothing. The highly polished gun had misfired, the trigger stopping at half cock. He could have stopped then since, technically, the trigger was pulled, and the duel would have been considered complete. Jackson, however, drew the hammer back a second time and fired. The bullet passed through Dickinson, dropping the young man to the ground.

Overton walked over to the unconscious man lying on the dewy grass. "He won't want anything more of you, General," he stated somberly, for only the general to hear.[14] When the men approached a spring on their way back from Harrison's Mill Landing, an obviously exhausted Jackson approached a woman churning butter and asked her for a drink. It was then that his doctor noticed the general's blood. "My God, General Jackson, are you hit?" exclaimed the concerned man. Not wanting to give his adversary's supporters any satisfaction, Jackson exclaimed, "Oh, I believe he has pinked me a little. Let's look at it but say nothing about it."[15] The fact was that Dickinson's bullet had indeed aimed true for the heart, and, if not for the general's coat, he would surely not have lived to accomplish the things for which history now remembers him. Andrew Jackson went to bed that night with a seared breastbone and several broken ribs. Not to mention the pain from the bullet he would carry in his body to the day he died, many years later.

* * * * * *

Jackson's star began to rise to national prominence shortly after his duel with Charles Dickinson, first through his military exploits at the Battle of New Orleans in the War of 1812, then Indian Wars, and finally through his seizure and governance of Florida. Ironically, when the war against Britain and its Native American allies came calling, Andrew Jackson was once more recovering from gunshot wounds—albeit milder than the one he received from Dickinson. At 46 years old in 1813, the statesman got involved in a tavern fight in Nashville with one Thomas H. Benton, later a Missouri senator, resulting in two slugs shot into his back by Benton's brother. He was still in a sling and recovering from his injuries when the government called upon him to fight the British-allied

Creek Indians. Hindered by his injuries, with the left sleeve of his coat empty and unable to climb into the saddle unassisted or ride long without stopping to be washed from head to toe in a solution of sugar of lead to keep down the inflammation, Jackson set out to become a national hero.[16]

In the next seven months, Andrew Jackson managed to win seven major victories as the general of the Tennessee militia in what became known as the Creek War, resulting in the acquisition of lands in Alabama and Georgia. After the victories against the Native American foe, Jackson was appointed major general in the regular army in May 1814. He continued his rise by expelling the British from Mobile and then Pensacola in September and November. Then came the Battle of New Orleans, which made him a household name. When the British sailed a massive fleet to capture the entrance to the Mississippi, Jackson's troops deprived the British of the advantage of their navy through well-planned fortifications, in turn making them attack the city by land and not by sea on January 8, 1815. Using what amounted to trench warfare, the American forces killed 2,117 British soldiers in a mere 23 minutes while losing no more than 13 men.[17]

Famed historian James Morgan stated that had there been no Battle of New Orleans, "there would have been no hero of New Orleans, and Jackson would never have been President."[18] Following the biggest triumph of his military career, Jackson's name began to be placed along with another acclaimed general, George Washington. The man who would become the first president born in a log cabin, who came into this world fatherless and homeless from poor Irish immigrant stock, who was practically raised by the U.S. military, and who taught himself law became the embodiment of the West's self-made man. He fell right into symbolizing the new-West struggle against the aristocratic East when, as a major general under President James Monroe, he invaded Spanish territory in Florida to pursue hostile Seminole Indians in 1821. When the invasion was denounced by the powers that were as an act of violence and an abuse of the authority granted to him by the president, Jackson's new status as a shunned westerner further fed his popularity among those seeing the political status quo in Washington, D.C., as undemocratic. As far as the new common man was concerned, Jackson's actions opened more land for the poor American whites to cultivate while safeguarding them from the Native American threat.

Bullets That Changed America

Yet, it would be the consequences of the election of 1824 that brought Andrew Jackson and the new democratic populist base closer together. The election for Monroe's successor showcased the bitter regional divisions within the United States following the Panic of 1819. This was not a contest of political parties as there was only one still in existence, the Republicans. Instead, this was a battle between the North, the South, and the West, with each region putting forth its favorite son. Jackson, the new embodiment of the West, was nominated not for his platform, for he had none, but for his persona and military accomplishments. And although he won the popular vote, the still hesitant statesman was turned into the champion of Western democracy by the corrupt political system in power. After the claims emerged of a corrupt bargain—where Congress, following a push from Henry Clay, gave the election, in which no one had a majority of the electoral votes, to the aristocratic John Quincy Adams, in return for the former receiving the post of the secretary of state—Jackson swore off the broken political establishment.

His supporters in all parts of the county kept up the narrative that Jackson had been unjustly deprived of the presidency as he received the largest number of electoral votes and popular votes. And so the propertyless masses—along with western farmers and northern factory workers—now with a loud voice in American politics, united behind their self-made man, who now also felt slighted by the establishment. When Jackson, this time at the head of the newly established Democratic Party, came back to run for president again in 1828, the democratic spirit had spread even to the original states. Morgan would write that "[even] in New England the village artisan and the poor farmer from the backcountry rose up in town meeting to challenge the squire and the parson."[19] Jackson's victory had ended the apparent dynasty of aristocrats and scholars from Virginia and New England.[20] The man pierced by a bullet at Harrison's Mill on the Red River in Logan, Kentucky, 22 years prior, was now a people's champion. A symbol of a changing America, in an era that would come to bear his name and leave a lasting impression on the political and social character of the nation forever.

Andrew Jackson symbolized the new American spirit of his followers, who began to call themselves Jacksonian Democrats. At its core, this new democracy introduced an altered paradigm about the relationship between the government and its people to the annals of American history. It stood for opening up the political process to more people—as long as they were not African American, Native American, or women. Richard Hofstadter perhaps defined it best when he called the Jacksonian presidency and movement a struggle of large sections of the American community against a political and business elite and its allies. "It grew out of expanding opportunities and a common desire to enlarge these opportunities still further by removing restrictions and privileges that had their origin in acts of government."[21]

Politics became a popular pastime that no longer excluded the majority of the population based on their economic or family status. Supporters held public rallies and parades in support of their hero, whom they christened "Old Hickory" because of his toughness and unwavering determination. Party functionaries reached out to every neighborhood with promises of jobs for supporters. Government posts, Jackson explained, should be easily accessed by the people, not reserved for a privileged class of permanent career politicians. Jackson would introduce the concept of office rotation, decried by his opponents as the spoils system, which saw that government went not only to those most qualified but also to those loyal to the party in power.

This feeling of political inclusiveness was further perpetuated by politics entering the popular media. Eric Foner described the nearly 400 Democratic and Whig papers being published in 1830—more than four times the number published in 1800: "Every significant town, it seemed, had [a newspaper], whose job was not so much to report the news as to present the party's position on the issues of the day [and those of their leaders]."[22] For the first time, national politics became a spectacle, a battle between those on one side of the issue versus those on the other. Not behind the closed doors of Congress but on the streets and in the homes of average Americans. Like their leader in the White House, the common people continued to exalt this new version of participatory democracy—a standard that was there to stay.

Jacksonian democracy was about creating political as well as economic opportunities. Through liberating capitalism from the clutches of the wealthy elites—e.g., the shareholders of the national bank who blocked the common man's access to credit—the new president attempted to create better opportunities for the average American. The idea was that only through equal access to wealth would a common man have a chance in politics as money and public office went hand in hand. Jackson refused to recharter the Second Bank of the United States. In doing so, he refused to support its shareholders, who, unlike average American taxpayers, earned interest from the federal tax revenue deposits. And although his subsequent division of national funds among smaller state banks would lead to a national economic depression, it introduced into the American system the idea of removing the federal government from the economy, which Eric Foner contended would allow ordinary Americans to test their abilities in the fair competition of a self-regulating market.[23]

It is equally hard to imagine what the office of the presidency would look like had it not been held by "King" Jackson in the 1830s. While the former presidents saw their job as mere executors of the will of Congress and respected the idea of checks and balances, Jackson's personality and style would alter that perception forever. Viewing senators and representatives as aristocratic, the seventh president saw legislative and executive branches on the same level and with the same rights to decide on laws. This attitude would see him veto more bills than all of his predecessors combined. Believing that the president, directly chosen by the people's will, was the true embodiment of democracy, Jackson saw himself as the people's true champion. His will was the will of the American people. At one point, he would even defy the Supreme Court with his remark, "[Justice] John Marshall has made his decision, now let him enforce it."[24] While his opponents saw him as a demagogue who bent to the will of the masses, to his supporters, Andrew Jackson and the office of the presidency became the only true face of government and democracy. The popular presidency was now a reality, as was the persona of a strong-willed leader—what some would later call an imperial president, a term used frequently to describe others with similar attitudes who followed in Jackson's footsteps. After all, they had a model.

Unquestionably, Jackson's legacy would forever be tarnished by what historian Kenneth C. Davis called "a new level of militant, land-frenzied, slavery condoning, Indian-killing greed." It would be impossible to say how different the future would have been for Native Americans had a prominent Indian fighter—known for his harsh treatment of Native Americans as general—not become president of the United States. One thing is certain: it was during Jackson's presidency and under his direction that popular anti–Indian sentiment and regional battles morphed into an official federal policy of Indian removal that continued past his two terms.[25] Some historians point to the humanitarian impetus behind the move as Jackson frequently spoke of the two races hindering one another's freedom. Others, such as Eric Foner, point to the slave states pressuring the government to access the Indian land and open it to more cotton cultivation. This was an attitude supported by Jackson's opponents at the time; Thomas Benton of Missouri saw the policy of Indian removal as nothing short of "extending the area to slavery" and "converting Indian soil into slave soil."[26] Regardless, there is no denying that Andrew Jackson's presidency had dire consequences for both the Native American and slave population of the United States.

So what would the United States look like had Andrew Jackson fallen from the bullet clearly meant for his heart in May 1806? Perhaps, the political movement would have come to fruition regardless and without its champion. Perhaps, but it is unlikely. What would the future of Native Americans look like had John Quincy Adams, who openly believed in the federal and state government's adherence to agreed-upon land treaties with Indians, continued as the president of the United States? Would the popular participatory democracy movement simply be absorbed into the Republican party with minor concessions instead of becoming a populist movement and its own political party? Would the American people tolerate strong or "imperial" presidents as easily a century later? Just perhaps, the United States would not have been what it became had Dickinson's bullet hit its mark.

FOR FURTHER READING

Although Andrew Jackson is but a mere chapter in a much more encompassing history of American politics, Richard Hofstadter's *The American Political Tradition* (1989) provides a great analysis of the politics of the seventh president. For an all-encompassing picture of Jackson's political life, one cannot go wrong with Jon Meacham's *American Lion: Andrew Jackson in the White House* (2008). For the context of the times and the rise of the new politically aware West, and to understand Jackson's role in the new populist movement, *The Early American Republic: 1789–1829* by Paul E. Johnson (2007), as well as *The Nation Takes Shape: 1789–1837* by Marcus Cunliffe (1959), serve the purpose well. For an overview of Jackson's effect on popular politics, *The Birth of Modern Politics: Andrew Jackson, John Quincy Adams, and the Election of 1828* (2009) by Lynn Hudson Parsons does a great job of covering the heated election in a short but jam-packed volume in the *Pivotal Moments in American History* series.

3

Death of a Prophet, October 5, 1813

There were men with tomahawks swarming around private James Knaggs. Others were scalping his brothers-in-arms. Gunshots tore into the Native Americans as they continued charging at the white soldiers. With the all-encompassing fog around him, Knaggs stumbled in the swampy ground under his feet. And then: "I distinctly heard his voice, with which I was perfectly familiar. He yelled like a tiger and urged on his braves to the attack."[1] The young private fell to the ground and attempted to quickly prime his musket, yet found the gun powder too wet to do him any good.

Knaggs rose and moved towards the sound of battle, swinging his weapon like a club, abandoning his futile attempt to reload it. And then he saw him, Colonel Johnson, "with one leg confined by the body of his white mare, which had been killed and had fallen upon him."[2] Knaggs ran towards his badly wounded commanding officer. Another private, and friend, Medard Labadie, was near them. Suddenly, the men abandoned trying to lift the fallen colonel, who was lying on his side panting. They noticed the gun still clenched in his hand as their gazes followed the direction of its muzzle. About 20 or 30 feet from the moaning officer was a Native American, "lying on his face, dead ... stretched at full length and shot through his body ... near the heart."[3] The tomahawk was near his outstretched right hand, its edge stuck in the ground and its brass pipe sticking up towards the sky.

Johnson drew their attention, calling out, "Knaggs, let me lay here, and push on."[4] But the boys did not listen. They freed their colonel from under his mount and wrapped him in a blanket. As they carried the barely conscious and copiously bleeding body of their fallen leader out of harm's way, the young privates were careful not to step over a body of a Native American lying nearby.

* * * * *

There is as much controversy and mystery surrounding the death of the Native American leader Tecumseh as there is about the exact location of his dead body. We may not know much, but we know enough. Author James C. Klotter perhaps said it best: "In 1813, a great Indian leader was shot and died. His name was Tecumseh (TA-KUM-SE). His life would become a legend."[5] The significance of the fallen leader's very existence and his death can be best summarized through the effects both had on the course of history. For William H. Harrison, the future U.S. president who famously fought the Shawnee leader, the unified Indian threat justified the seizure of Native American lands and the overall territorial expansion into Indian territory in the northwest. To the observer of the greater context of history, the death of Tecumseh signaled the end of Native American resistance in the East, forcing the depleted tribes across the Mississippi and

TECUMSEH.

The Shawnee chief Tecumseh fought a long war against the United States expansion only to fall to the Americans during the War of 1812, before his dream of a unified Native American confederacy could be realized (Library of Congress).

setting up the ultimate showdown that would bring about the end of Native Americans' freedom as they knew it. It would also set up precedents for dealing with armed Indian resistance and military conflicts that would become known as the "Indian Wars." Ironically, it would also propel to the White House a man whose death would indirectly lead to the annexation of Texas, the eventual Mexican–American War, and the fulfillment of America's manifest destiny. The latter, of course, would not only bring Tecumseh's struggle to its ultimate conclusion but also shape the world that we know today.

Henry Clay's War Hawks secured the control of the House of Representatives in 1810–1811. With the U.S. blaming the British for the impressment of American sailors on the high seas and for provoking Indian raids on the American frontier, the two nations were once again on a collision course. Yet, concurrent with the greater conflict between the Crown and the young United States that would become known as the War of 1812 was another source of trouble brewing between the U.S. and its closest neighbors, the Native Americans. When, in 1809, Indiana Territory's governor, William Henry Harrison, persuaded several tribal leaders to sign away over three million tribal acres to the U.S. government, not all chiefs gave in. One particular young leader believed that the only protection against the encroachment of whites onto Native American lands centered on creating a great Indian confederacy. His name was Tecumseh.

The charismatic leader was nearly six feet tall with a lighter complexion than that of his peers. According to various accounts, he did not have any tattoos, which was the norm for other Shawnee members of his tribe, and carried himself in a very commanding matter. His name evoked the image of a panther leaping across the sky like a shooting star.[6] Shortly after the turn of the nineteenth century, the young leader, already famous for his bravery and intellect, caught the eye of American leadership when he began a reform movement to cast off white civilization from Native American tribal lands. Tecumseh's famous enemy, William H. Harrison, called him one of "those uncommon geniuses which spring up occasionally to ... overturn the established order of things," adding that the young leader might have founded in other circumstances an empire rivaling the Aztecs and Incas.[7]

Embarking on the four-year quest to spread his message of unity, the Shawnee chief attempted to do something that no Native American had ever accomplished. The repercussions of his potential success would be catastrophic for the American government's plans of westward expansion. Starting in Ohio and going as far as Florida, Tecumseh spent the years between 1807 and 1811 attempting to unite tribes into one Native American nation—an entity that would cast off white oppression and its threat against the Indian way of life. Speaking to the Choctaw and the Chickasaw leadership, the young chief proclaimed, "Indians must form one body, one heart and defend to the last warrior our country, our homes, our liberty and the graves of our fathers."[8] The new threat, Tecumseh said, transcended old tribal divisions. This was not about being a Pawnee, Osage, Quapaw, Caddo, or even Cherokee, Choctaw, Chickasaw, Creek, or Seminole—this was about survival.

Together with his younger brother, known to the whites as the Prophet, the men warned against the Native Americans' reliance on white men's way of life—particularly the consumption of alcohol—angering the Great Spirit. The time to correct that mistake was now. The chief's news began to spread, and soon, the Ohio River Valley tribes—the Shawnees, Miamis, Mingos, Kickapoos, Ottawas, Potawatomi, Wyandots, and Delawares—joined his cause. The United States authorities were alarmed. If Tecumseh was successful, the young nation, already on the verge of a new war with Britain, could never win a decisive victory against a unified Native American force along the entire frontier. The movement needed to stop before it got going, before—heaven forbid—it led to enough small victories to inspire a greater uprising and following.

Elliott West, an American historian and author summarized the great Shawnee chief's significance to American history when he wrote:

> On the eve of the War of 1812, Tecumseh represented the last best hope of American Indians to preserve ways of life they had known for centuries as white settlers sought to make their own dreams a reality on the frontier. The fate of hundreds of thousands of Indians of that era and for centuries to come rested on his shoulders as he built the greatest pan-Indian confederation the westward nation would ever confront. Tecumseh was a man of extraordinary foresight, whose vision rivaled that of the founders of the young republic. But his saga would end in tragedy—for him personally and for the Indians as a whole.[9]

The road to Tecumseh's equally mysterious and painful death began in 1811 when the young chief, seeing the war between Britain and the U.S.

as inevitable, started his negotiations with the Crown. Unbeknownst to him, the events that followed would lead to his downfall and the collapse of American Indians' best hope of stopping their complete destruction at the hands of the Americans.

In November of 1811, Tecumseh's younger brother used his older sibling's temporary absence to test the still green and growing pan–Indian confederation. Despite orders from the chief to avoid any fighting, the Prophet mounted a sneak attack on Harrison's forces on the banks of the Tippecanoe River. While the elder sibling was on his quest to gather more supporters from the Southern states, the younger brother directed his men as they snuck up on the sleeping U.S. forces camped out nearby. The Native Americans attacked three times, and three times they were pushed back by the quickly mobilized professional troops under Harrison's command. Demoralized, the warriors retreated to their settlement. But by then, the future president had had enough. Harrison followed his foe to their capital, known as Prophetstown, and burned it to the ground in a day that saw much carnage on both sides. It was a painful victory, more like a tie. Harrison ended the day with 61 dead and with so many wounded—127—that he had to burn supplies to make room for the injured men in the covered wagons used for ambulances.[10] As much as it was a terrible psychological setback for Tecumseh and his efforts and dreams towards a great tribal unity, the battle would become the single most important event in William Henry Harrison's ascendance to the White House 30 years later.

It was also this event that finally convinced the reluctant Tecumseh to join his efforts with those of the British. While such a move seemed at odds with the non-white alliance he advocated, the British promised him a separate Native American state. To the British, having the Indians control the upper Ohio River Valley would have created a perfect buffer zone between the growing aspirations of the Americans and their remaining interests in Canada. Ironically, it was this new relationship that finally drove the British and Americans into war. Blaming the British for arming the Indians and inciting frontier attacks, the War Hawks in the U.S. Congress finally pushed the nation to war. For them, as for many Americans at the time, this war was not about world affairs but the control of the western frontier and the possible acquisition of Canada. This was to be a war for land.

Yet everything soon fell apart. England, still fighting against

France's Napoleon, saw the war with the U.S. as an unneeded distraction. And apart from one decisive American victory at the Battle of New Orleans—which incidentally took place after the war was already over because the commanders of the two sides had not yet gotten the news—and some American naval victories, the war was nothing more than a draw for the two nations. Even though the Americans failed to meet their goals of taking over Canada, they did manage to win the frontier war by crushing Indian resistance. And by the end of the conflict, both nations were just happy for it to end regardless of any gains. As for Tecumseh, his forces, now allied with the British, failed to protect and reclaim their lands in the Ohio territory, now in complete control of Harrison's forces. Still, he did not break his vow to support his allies, who by 1813 were in full retreat from the area. It was Tecumseh's insistence on protecting the British through their withdrawal in the waning months of the western war that the Shawnee chief found himself at the battle of Thames River in upper Canada. October 5, 1813, was a cold and misty Tuesday.

* * * * * *

Richard Mentor Johnson stood, evaluating the foggy field in front of him. With a river on the left and a large swamp on the right, the area was not wide enough for a frontal cavalry assault. Hidden in the distance by the murky weather were the British and their Indian allies under the command of the great Shawnee chief Tecumseh. It was not possible to take the two divisions together. Johnson knew he would have to split his forces and attack them separately; his commanding officer William H. Harrison had all but ordered it. There was nobody he trusted more to attack the redcoats than his brother James Johnson. In turn, Richard would take his battalion of Kentuckian Dragoons and charge the Native Americans.

Harrison had initially planned to use his infantry in a frontal assault against the British. Still, his enemy used geography so skillfully that it forced the American general to rethink his strategy. Under the command of Major General Procter, the redcoats made a defensive line in the narrow space between the Thames River and a bog, while Tecumseh's forces took the swamp itself. As the bugle sounded, James Johnson's mounted division, swinging tomahawks like sabers, rushed the British line, breaking it in less than 10 minutes.[11] Procter became so frightened that he ordered his forces to retreat, himself at the helm. In pursuit, the Americans did not get the British general, but they did take hundreds of prisoners and captured about $1 million in supplies.[12]

Watching the British defeat unfold in front of their eyes, Tecumseh and his warriors waited in the trees until the American horsemen were within a few yards of them. And then they poured in their heavy fire. Within seconds, gunfire emptied an estimated 20 saddles. Wounded within the first minutes of the battle, Richard Johnson ordered his soldiers to dismount and follow the Indians into the woods on foot. As they pushed forward, Tecumseh's forces counter-charged instead of retreating. Through the massive confusion and the heavy fog, a 64-year-old colonel William Whitley snapped to attention as a Native American charged at him with a gun. Both men fired and fell almost simultaneously to the ground, dead. Nearby, Richard Johnson, slumping from his saddle and bleeding from his wounds, spurred his soldiers on.

Then he heard the cry and his head snapped. In his account published in 1859, Isaac Hamblin claimed to be standing near Johnson when he shot Tecumseh.

> Johnson's horse fell under him, he himself being also deeply wounded; in the fall he lost his sword, his large pistols were empty, and he was entangled with his horse in the ground. Tecumseh had fired his rifle at him, and when he saw him fall, he threw down his gun and bounded forward like a tiger, sure of his prey. Johnson had only a side pistol ready for use. He aimed at the chief, over the head of his horse, and shot near the center of his forehead. When the ball struck, it seemed that the Indian jumped with his head full fifteen feet into the air; as soon as he struck the ground, a little Frenchman ran his bayonet into him, and pinned him fast to the ground.

In one of these two encounters, Whitley's and Johnson's, Tecumseh was shot dead. As the men near Johnson were too preoccupied with getting their commanding officer out of the carnage, they left the bodies of the two shot Indians behind. Historians may not agree which was Tecumseh, but they do agree that the Shawnee leader died in the forest during the battle. Johnson himself never claimed the credit for shooting the great Indian chief, but his supporters did during the election of 1836, which saw him become the vice president of the United States.

While a few others claimed to have shot Tecumseh on that day, the bigger mystery revolved around his body and its final burial place.

The Battle of the Thames, which led to the death of the Native American leader Tecumseh, as painted by A. Chappel. Although accounts differ, this depiction credited Colonel Richard Johnson as the one who fired the fatal shot in Ontario, Canada, on October 5, 1813 (Library of Congress).

At the scene of the battle, where, yards apart from each other, Whitley and Johnson had each shot a Native American, a fallen Indian was identified as Tecumseh by a scar on the left side of his face and one leg shorter than the other. Also of interest was the fact that the body had a fatal wound to the left breast—consistent with either being shot by Whitley or stabbed by the bayonet as described in Johnson's version of events—as well as an unspecified wound to the head, also consistent with both accounts. In at least one account, in the excitement of their discovery, soldiers began to peel strips of skin from the cadaver to take home, leaving the body badly mutilated. The body was then grouped with other Indian casualties and buried in a mass grave. This, of course, is just one version of what happened. In another, Tecumseh's followers got to the body before the American soldiers did and managed to bury it in a secret grave. What is undisputed is the fact that the great Indian leader was shot and died on that day. The Battle of the Thames crushed the British-Indian coalition forever and with it dreams of an independent Indian nation. From Ohio to Minnesota, the entire Midwest was thrown open to American occupation, and Indiana and Illinois became states in 1816 and 1818, respectively.[13] Subsequently shattered was Tecumseh's vision of a powerful pan-Indian confederacy, clearing the way for an unstoppable onslaught of white settlers and the permanent removal of Indians from their native lands.[14]

* * * * * *

The now infamous relocation of the Cherokee Indians, known as the Trail of Tears, was, in essence, the culmination of the events that transpired after the death of Tecumseh. Even before the 1830 Indian Removal Act, which saw the removal of the remaining tribal nations to the east and across the Mississippi River into designated reservations, many Native Americans already saw the futility in resisting white expansion. For many, the ability to retain their culture and autonomy relied on being away from U.S. settlers. And despite lack of any fanfare, one by one tribes negotiated treaties with the U.S., which resulted in ceding land claims to the U.S. government. In return, the Native Americans were promised a peaceful transition across the Mississippi River into today's Oklahoma, an area then known simply as Indian Territory. According to the National Park Service website in 2020, more than 200 treaties were forced on tribes, establishing nearly a hundred reservations west of the great river.[15] That is not to say that all tribes went peacefully. The period encompassed the Creek War, which began concurrently with Harrison's force battling Tecumseh, and the Seminole Wars, which resulted from the U.S. acquisition of Florida from Spain.

In the short term, historian John Sugden probably best sums up Tecumseh's death and the overall British failure at the Battle of the Thames:

> [Tecumseh's] was the last great battle to be fought in a theater that had been a vortex of conflict for more than half a century, a tradition embracing the French and Indian War, Pontiac's uprising, the Revolution, and the Northwestern Indian War, as well as the War of 1812. No more were Indian and white armies to march in common cause over the great Northwest; no longer were the natives of those wide regions to defend their birthright in a

major battle; never again were the Indians of North America an international force, affecting the imperialist adventures of the great nations. They were merely a domestic problem of no great import to national security.[16]

The bullet that struck the Shawnee chief, whether it came from William Whitley, Richard Johnson, or one of the other men who would claim years later to have slain the great leader, marked a defining moment in the nation's frontier history. The northern chapter of the conflict between Indians and white settlers had come to an end.

There were also some unforeseen and less obvious effects on the overall Native American experience that came out of that Tuesday in October of 1813. William Henry Harrison, the general in charge of the offensive against the British and Tecumseh's Indian forces, rode the fame from his victories to the presidency in 1840. Nicknamed "Old Tippecanoe," Harrison and his running mate, John Tyler, are immortalized in high school textbooks as "Tippecanoe and Tyler Too." Yet, his death just 31 days into his first term also made his term the shortest of any president in American history. Something that, no doubt, he would not have wanted to be remembered for.

The significance of his death does not merely lie in the first transition of the vice president into the head position after the death of a presiding head of state. In this case, it is the fact that John Tyler was the person that was doing the taking over. Not really liked by his constituents and chosen to run on Harrison's ticket primarily to garner Southern votes for the still reasonably new Whig Party, Tyler set into motion the events that would eventually lead to the complete national submission of Native Americans. If it were not for Harrison, Tyler would never have been placed in position nor had enough power and influence when president of the United States. Ignored by the Democratic Party and not exactly in line with the activist economic and pro-national bank programs of the Northern Whigs, John Tyler was in the right place at the right time. Being a prominent Virginian and an outspoken opponent of Presidents Jackson and Van Buren, the senator, although not a perfect fit, landed on the ticket next to Harrison. Nearly a century after Tyler's presidency ended, historian David Muzzey stated: "John Tyler, of Virginia, was named for Vice-President, simply to get votes in the South; for Tyler was a states-rights man [whereas Whigs were ardent Federalists], an anti–Bank man [the main agenda of the Whig party being the preservation of a national bank], and a low-tariff man [whereas high tariffs, especially on foreign goods, were fundamental to Whig Party ideology], whose only bond of sympathy with the Whigs was hatred for Andrew Jackson."[17]

Although often viewed as a tragic, accidental, and disliked president—every member of his cabinet except his secretary of state resigned within the first five months of his term—his one term in office had a lasting impact on Native Americans. First came the Preemption Act of 1841, which permitted squatters living on federal government-owned western lands to purchase up to 160 acres at a meager price before the land was offered for sale to the general public. The law spurred many people to venture west onto federal lands, often ignoring past treaties that granted some of those lands to various Native American tribes. Still, no single event would have a bigger effect on the fate of Native Americans in the U.S. than the Mexican–American War. This in turn led to the acquisition by the U.S. of all western territories and hence the fulfillment of the expansionists' manifest destiny—an empire that stretched from sea to shining sea. Any historian who studies American history will undoubtedly point to the acquisition of Texas as the catalyst for the said events, which would lead to millions of Americans venturing west into lands formerly designated for Native Americans. And it just so happens that it was John Tyler who, knowing he would never be re-elected president and would not have to deal with the repercussions, pushed the unpopular annexation of Texas through Congress. The rest, as they say, is history.

For Further Reading

Written by Benjamin Drake, one of the earliest works chronicling Tecumseh's life and death is *Life of Tecumseh and His Brother the Prophet* (1850). While it lacks the perspective of time, the short book details the Native American leader's life as well as his war against the white people. It also provides a detailed and well-researched account of the Battle of Tippecanoe. A more modern retelling of the leader's life and one that considers the historiography on the topic is John Sugden's *Tecumseh: A Life* (2013). Random House published the most recent work on the topic in 2020. Titled *Tecumseh and the Prophet: The Shawnee Brothers Who Defied a Nation* (2020), Peter Cozzens's work—as the title suggests—concentrates more on the relationship between Tecumseh and the Prophet rather than their military campaign. For a more detailed account of the eastern military conflicts between the Native

Americans and the settlers one should turn to Robert M. Owens's *"Indian Wars" and the Struggle for Eastern North America, 1763–1843* (2021), which includes not only an analysis of the conflict but also a plethora of primary documents relating to the struggle. And while you are at it, Owens's *Mr. Jefferson's Hammer: William Henry Harrison and the Origins of American Indian Policy* (2007) presents a very "popular history" account of the wars against Tecumseh, which reads more like an action novel and not a work of non-fiction.

4

They Came in the Night, May 28, 1856

The party of eight men crept across Mosquito Creek near the junction with the Pottawatomie River in Kansas. Although part of the group, James Townsley was closely watched by two men on each side of him who questioned his commitment to the cause. Their arrival at the property of a Southern gentleman James knew well from childhood was briefly interrupted by a loud dog promptly silenced with a slash of a saber by one of the men. As one group set the house ablaze, Townsley watched additional men enter the cabin and force out the elderly owner and his two young sons.

The party then marched their captives half a mile away from the fire and ordered them to a stop. Without any apparent remorse, the gang leader placed the gun right to the forehead of the pleading father and pulled the trigger. Almost instantly, two men from the posse hacked down the remaining two sons with their short swords right where they stood. John Brown put his gun away and ordered the reluctant James Townsley to point them towards the next house.

The bullet that the 56-year-old John Brown fired that night would mark the beginning of a set of events that would escalate the tensions between the North and the South to an irreversible breakdown of national unity. As the men marched into the night seeking another home, they were setting into motion three months of local carnage, resulting in more than 200 deaths—in what newspapers would call "Bleeding Kansas." A chapter in a much larger struggle that witnessed the killing along the Kansas and Missouri border spread to the whole nation and would go on for another decade.

* * * * * *

Bullets That Changed America

When the United States ratified the Constitution in 1787, the northern and southern regions of the nation were political equals. At least in the sense that when counting for congressional representation, the South made up for its low population numbers through the mutually agreed upon three-fifths compromise, which counted each slave as three-fifths of a person for census purposes. The Senate also maintained an equilibrium, with both regions having an equal number of states, thus keeping the balance of pro- and anti-slavery states. Yet, all of that was about to change. Spurred on by the ever-growing European immigration to the U.S., by the 1850s, the Northern population growth outpaced its Southern counterpart enough to where past compromises would no longer suffice. As the idea of manifest destiny pushed more Americans west, new states began to vie for statehood, only further threatening the already sensitive balance. There were also no more illusions as to which region had more representation in Congress.

Following the latest compromise meant to mollify national distress—known as the Compromise of 1850—the issue of the South maintaining its already dissipating influence in Congress boiled to the surface once again. And this time, there would be no quelling it. Developed by Stephen Douglas of Illinois—whom Abraham Lincoln would famously defeat in the 1860 presidential election—a plan was put forth in 1854 to divide, develop, and organize the vast unoccupied territory west of Iowa and Missouri. Douglas believed that popular sovereignty, where people of a given area would vote on whether to allow or disallow slavery in their territory and state, would be most fitting for the two new territories of Kansas and Nebraska. The implications of the proposed Kansas-Nebraska Act of 1854 were even greater as it left the door open to the spread of slavery into Northern territories in the Union—something held at bay through the U.S. Constitution, the Missouri Compromise, and the Compromise of 1850. Considering the bitterness coming out of the issue, the bill passed Congress and became law in 1854. Undoubtedly with the help of the expansionist President Franklin Pierce, a fellow Democrat.

The race for possession of Kansas was on, and New York senator William Seward took on the challenge: "Come on, then, gentlemen of the Slave States ... we will engage in competition for the virgin soil of Kansas and God give the victory to the side that is stronger in numbers as it is in the right."[1] The rate at which settlers poured into Kansas was unprecedented. Within mere months, the territory had enough settlers to petition the federal government for an election. By March 1855, it was time to see if Kansas would become free or slave. Unfortunately, there would be enough disputed evidence pointing to the legality of the election that it is difficult to say to this day what the true results were. What we do know is that thousands of armed men known as "border ruffians" from the slave state of Missouri, led by Missouri senator David Atchison, crossed into Kansas to vote illegally before returning to their state.[2]

Winning the fraudulent election, the pro-slavery government set itself up in the town of Lecompton and wasted no time in passing acts favoring the peculiar institution. Not to be outdone, the pro-abolitionist faction of the state, not agreeing with the election results, set up their anti-slavery government in Topeka. Inevitably, when President Pierce recognized the legitimacy—or rather the illegitimacy—of the election results, violence in the state became inevitable. When an anti-slavery man attempted to assassinate a pro-slavery sheriff as he rode his horse into the abolitionist town of Lawrence to arrest a murderer, the stage was set for an incident.[3] A posse of nearly one thousand pro-slavery armed men descended on the town on May 21, 1856. By the time they left, the anti-slavery headquarters building was a pile of dust, as were two newspaper presses and many homes; many more were looted. The event caught the eye of John Brown, a recent arrival to Kansas. Within a day, the 56-year-old Connecticut man was on his way to right the wrongs of Lawrence. The war of words between the North and the South was about to turn into one of blood and bullets.

John Brown was by every definition an idealist. Proclaiming himself chosen by God to fight against slavery, the financially unsuccessful father and husband moved to a black community farm of a wealthy abolitionist Gerrit Smith, at North Elba, New York, in 1849. There, Brown continued to support abolitionist causes and help finance escaped slaves' transition to freedom. After arriving in Kansas with his five sons in 1855 to partake in the elections, the ardent abolitionist was shocked by what he viewed as complacency on the part of the anti-slavery movement. In May 1856, he joined one of the free-state volunteer companies, the Pottawatomie Rifles, to protect the town of Lawrence, which he heard was raided. But before they reached their destination, they had learned that the town was already sacked and that the United States troops were now in charge.[4] The following day, Brown managed to persuade seven members of his group—which included four of his sons and a son-in-law—to avenge the five abolitionists who had lost their lives during the sacking of Lawrence. Unbeknownst to Brown, his information about the five deaths had been incorrect. This, however, did not matter to the five men whom, in the next 24 hours, Brown and his followers would kill in revenge.

* * * * * *

Just shy of 41 years old, James Townsley was already a veteran of the Second Seminole War and the Creek War. Through his enlistment with the Second United States Dragoons, the man had witnessed some of the most bitter and violent fighting the frontier had to offer. He could still see the blood, the carnage, and the scalps whenever he closed his eyes. But none of that mattered now. Having retired after the Mexican–American War and taken up house painting as a profession, James could not have foreseen how his decision to move himself and his wife to Kansas in 1855 would impact the rest of his life. He settled in Anderson County, on the Pottawatomie Creek, and Townsley's neighbors recruited him to join the Pottawatomie Rifles because of his past military experience. It was there that he met his new captain, one John Brown, Jr., the eldest son of the more infamous John Brown.

James thought the old man Brown was mad. They had just learned of the sacking of Lawrence when the elder Brown approached him. "He wanted to know if I would take my team and take him and his boys back so that they could keep watch of what was going on," he later recalled.[5] The man agreed. After all, they were heading towards his hometown, and God only knew he longed to see his wife. It had been weeks since he joined the abolitionist group initially called up to counter the growing influx of Border Ruffians during the election period. The election was lost, as was their cause, and he knew it was time to go home. His new leader, however, had different plans. The party consisting of old John Brown, Frederick Brown, Owen Brown, Watson Brown, Oliver Brown, Henry Thompson (Brown's son-in-law), and one Mr. Winter set off towards their destination on May 24, 1856.

Having traveled for a full day, the men settled down to rest. After supper, James watched as "Old Man" Brown approached him.

4. They Came in the Night, May 28, 1856

Something was wrong. "John Brown told me for the first time what he proposed to do," the young man remembered. "He said he wanted me to pilot the company up to the forks of the creek some five or six miles above, into the neighborhood in which I lived, and show them where all the pro-slavery men resided; that he proposed to sweep the creek as he came down, of all pro-slavery men living on it."[6] James was frightened. He knew the people that Brown was talking about. He would not do it. Angry, old Brown kept the men camped out for another day. Then, as soon as darkness fell, Brown ordered his bewildered team to march. James knew where they were going.

Doyle's family home was in a field removed from the dirt road, making it a perfect location for anyone who wanted to approach it unnoticed. After killing a dog that came out of nowhere to protect its master's property, old John Brown and three of his sons—as well as his son-in-law—forced their way into the house. James wanted to run, but he knew that Frederick Brown was not just standing near him for fun. Townsley did not fail to notice the younger Brown's hand resting on the hilt of his short sword. The man was guarding him. Shortly, the posse members forced the older Doyle and his two younger sons out of their home at gunpoint. The younger men did not speak. Their father, however, was pleading for his kids' lives. The company, James included, marched away from the house. Apart from the bright half-moon and some low lighting coming from a couple of lanterns, the scene could not have been darker when the men were ordered to stop.

John Brown close to what he looked like during the Pottawatomie massacre. The man would become infamous for his raid on Harpers Ferry attempting to incite a slave rebellion (created in 1884, Library of Congress).

Years later, James Townsley vividly remembered the moment that even his time on the frontier could not have prepared him for. "Old John Brown drew his revolver and shot the old man Doyle in the forehead, and the two young-est [Brown] sons immediately fell upon the younger Doyles with their short two-edged swords."[7] One of the Doyle sons, still alive, attempted to crawl/walk away from the carnage, only to be mocked and promptly beheaded. The Pottawatomie massacre had begun.

The posse next marched down Mosquito Creek to the home of Allen Wilkinson, where once again James was guarded by the young Frederick Brown as the remainder of the party forced Wilkinson out of his cottage. "Wilkinson was taken, marched some distance south of the house, and slain in the road with a short sword by one of the younger Browns," recalled Townsley. As they walked into the night, the men could hear the loud sobbing of Wilkinson's wife as she sat on the ground sullied by blood, holding her husband's hacked skull in her hands. Brown's men "then crossed the Pottawatomie and came to the house of Henry Sherman," where once again James was forced to watch Sherman's younger brother—on the account that Henry was not home—being marched to the river, "where he was slain with swords by Brown's two youngest sons."[8] By the time the Browns were done with Sherman, his arm lay severed from his lifeless body, and his head was barely attached to the neck by the last remnants of some skin and liga-ments. "I did not approve of the killings," stated Townsley, "but Brown said it must be done for the protection of the Free State settlers; that the pro-slavery party must be terrified and that it was better that a score of bad men should die than that one man who came here to make Kan-sas a free State should be driven out."[9] Before departing the last house, the posse drove off the slain man's horses and then rode off to rejoin the Pottawatomie Rifles. John Brown was not yet done with his holy quest to see slavery eradicated from his nation. But at least now he knew the people would pay attention to his message when he was ready to provide one once more.

* * * * * *

Historian David M. Potter later wrote: "The Pottawatomie Massa-cre, combined as it was with the sack of Lawrence, brought both sides in Kansas to the belief that civil war was upon them and that they must kill their adversaries or be killed by them."[10] In essence, Kansas became the first battlefield of the nation's Civil War, years before the official declaration of the conflict. Perhaps not so ironically, John Brown would become one of the final nails in the coffin, so to speak, when looking at the eventual rupture between the North and the South.

Many events transpired between the Pottawatomie massacre and John Brown's attack on Harpers Ferry in 1859 that together make up the narrative of the short-term causes of the American Civil War. There is the caning of Senator Sumner by a pro-slavery congressman on the Senate floor; the Dred Scott decision, which revealed the national consensus about the non-human status of slaves; and the Abraham Lincoln and Stephen Douglas debates for a senatorial seat in Illinois, which would establish the former as the frontrunner of the newly created abolitionist Republican Party. Yet, one of the last events that led to the war involved the same man who caused the event that might have started the sectionalist violence in the first place.

After the massacre in Kansas, Brown went into hiding, yet his actions led to a certain following, specifically by wealthy supporters from New England, the epicenter of the abolitionist movement. Members of the group of ministers, educators, and landowners known as the Secret Six all had one thing in common: wealth. In 1858, the men met with Brown and agreed to his plan to march south, arm the slaves who would flock to his crusade, and establish a black republic in the Appalachians to wage war against the slaveholding South.[11] By this time, President James Buchanan had recognized Brown as a terrorist and offered a reward of $250 for his capture. The Pottawatomie massacre had not gone unnoticed. Had it not been for his showmanship in Kansas, Brown would not have gotten the necessary financial backing for his next endeavor. And it would be his new foray into Harpers Ferry that *The Richmond Enquirer* would call out in 1859 to have "advanced the cause of Disunion more than any other event ... since the formation of government. It has rallied to that standard of men who formerly looked upon it with horror; it has revived, with tenfold strength, the desire of a Southern Confederacy." The article all but predicted the disunion and Civil War that would follow John Brown's last raid. "The most determined friends of the Union may now be heard saying, 'If under the form of a [United States] our peace is disturbed, our state invaded, its peaceful citizens cruelly murdered ... by those who should be our warmest friends, ... and the people of the North sustain the outrage, then let the disunion come.'"[12]

Having assembled a band of 20 armed followers with the roughly $4,000 collected from his Northern backers, John Brown was ready to conclude his quest, which began with the attacks at Pottawatomie Creek. On October 16, 1859, the men attacked the federal arsenal at Harpers Ferry, Virginia (now West Virginia), with the intent of stirring up a slave rebellion that Brown would then turn into a full insurrection against the supporters of slavery. Yet as the men holed up in the arsenal building with hostages, the slaves who Brown expected to arrive never came to join him. News of the insurrection had spread before the attack commenced, and fearing repercussions from their masters, the slaves chose not to get involved. Subsequently, the local militia was ready for Brown, unraveling his conspiracy before it could take hold. The now-famous commanding officer of that militia, Colonel Robert E. Lee—who would go on to lead the Confederate forces in the American Civil War—easily defeated the holed-up men and arrested all those that survived the assault, Brown included.

The following month John Brown was tried for treason in a Virginia court and, entering no defense but his divine commission, was hastily condemned and hanged.[13] In the eyes of the Southerners, he was the embodiment of abolitionist fanaticism and the North's campaign to incite a slave rebellion supported by the Republican leadership. It only further strengthened the South's resolve when abolitionists such as Henry David Thoreau, Ralph Waldo Emerson, and Theodore Parker glorified Brown as a martyr. Thoreau even compared the man to Christ himself.[14] In retrospect, perhaps the Southern plantation class was on to something, especially when they eventually saw Northern regiments march through the South during the Civil War singing, "John Brown's body lies a-moldering in the grave, His soul goes marching on."

The South had quickly seized upon the John Brown raids in Pottawattamie and at Harpers Ferry as a weapon with which to criticize the newly growing Republican Party of which Abraham Lincoln was an aspiring presidential candidate. "Some of you admit that no Republican designated, aided or encouraged the Harpers Ferry affair, but still insist that our doctrines and declarations necessarily lead to such results," stated presidential candidate Lincoln to a sophisticated eastern audience at Cooper Union in New York City. "We do not believe it ... slave insurrections are no more common now that they were before the Republican Party was organized,"[15] he added. Regardless of the validity of his argument, it was too late to change the minds of the Southern proponents of secession. To them, John Brown was a product of the Republican Party's affiliation with the Northern abolitionist movement. Brown's heinous deeds, concurrent with the support the man received after his death from that Northern faction, convinced many that the ascendance of a Republican to the office of the presidency of the United States would be a direct threat to their way of life.

Henry Clay's message delivered in a speech before the United States Senate nearly 30 years before the unraveling of the Union now seemed like a prophecy foretold:

> The abolitionists, let me suppose, succeed in their present aim of uniting the inhabitants of the free states ... against the inhabitants of the slave states. Union on one side will beget union on the other. And this process of reciprocal consolidation will be attended with all the violent prejudices, embittered passions, and implacable animosities ... a virtual disunion of the Union will have taken place.... One section will stand in menacing and hostile array against the other. The collision of opinion will be quickly followed by the clash of arms.[16]

And thus, John Brown became that final wedge in the eventual disunion of the great American nation. To the South, he symbolized the radicalization of the North that could no longer be stopped. The election of Abraham Lincoln, the head of the Republican Party that was seen as a safe haven for abolitionists, would spell disaster. John Brown saw to it that the true intentions of the North, its political party, and the abolitionist movement, were now revealed for everyone to see.

In simplest terms, had old man Brown not fired a shot into Doyle's brain in October of 1856 near the Pottawattamie Creek, he would never have become the martyr for radical change that he ultimately became. More importantly, he would not have received the recognition that came from it and thus the support of the wealthy class of Northern abolitionists. This, in turn, would have taken away his ability to attempt to spark a slave rebellion in Harpers Ferry and thus would have dissolved the existence of the very event that would officially have the South fully distrust the North and its Republican party. A political institution they held responsible for inciting abolitionist ideas. This, regardless of Lincoln's personal and honest denial of the party's role in the Brown raids.

In a larger context, the killing of the five men by John Brown near Pottawatomie had an even greater role in sparking the eventual Civil

War. The massacre had undisputedly started months of carnage and civil war within the State of Kansas. The events of those three months led to the disenfranchisement of the pro-slavery faction in the state, which by 1857 had anti-slavery proponents outnumbering advocates of slavery, 10 to 1.[17] Thus, when President Buchanan endorsed a proslavery Lecompton Constitution that came out from the capital that many citizens viewed as illegitimate and sealed the admittance of Kansas to the Union as a slave state, the people felt betrayed.

One person in particular who saw this as a setback for the nation was a prominent Illinois Democratic senator, Stephen Douglas. The congressman's stance on the issue, specifically his endorsement of popular sovereignty over the fraudulent pro-slavery constitution, went against the overall position of the largely pro-slavery Democratic Party. The result of such a prominent member going against the Lecompton Constitution planted the seeds for the splintering of the Democratic Party into two regional factions. While the Northerners viewed Douglas as a hero, Southerners disdained him as a traitor. When the Democratic Party nominated Stephen Douglas for the presidential ticket in 1860, Southern Democrats left the convention. This split in the party opened the door for the worst possible scenario for the South. On November 6, 1860, voters went to the polls and elected Abraham Lincoln, a Republican who garnered less than 40 percent of the popular vote. Before his inauguration, 11 Southern states seceded from the Union. John Brown's quest to free the slaves and punish the slave owners, which began on a warm May evening in 1856, was about to enter its final chapter.

* * * * *

"I am quite certain that the crimes of this guilty land will never be purged away but with blood."—John Brown

FOR FURTHER READING

One of the most popular accounts of the legend of John Brown was written by none other than the early civil rights proponent and anti-abolitionist W.E.B. Dubois. Titled *John Brown: A Biography* (1909), the book relies on long quotations and may be more difficult to read for today's audience. Nonetheless, it is a very detailed account of Brown from his impoverished upbringing through his eventual anti-slavery crusade. Another book that may seem a bit more accessible to the reading public is David S. Reynolds's *John Brown, Abolitionist: The Man Who Killed Slavery, Sparked the Civil War, and Seeded Civil Rights* (2006). Especially of interest to those who found this chapter interesting would be Reynolds's own extremely detailed chapter on the Pottawatomie massacre, titled "Pottawatomie." For a more contextual read that places John Brown in the context of the greater so-called "impending crisis" preceding the Civil War, I would turn to David M. Potter's Pulitzer Prize-winning book *The Impending Crisis: America Before the Civil War, 1848–1861* (2011). And for those who want to spend the time, there is no better place to go to for Civil War history than Shelby Foote's three-volume masterpiece, *The Civil War: A Narrative* (1986).

5

"Halt, Who Goes There?"
May 2, 1863

It was 9:00 p.m. and the woods around Major John Decatur Barry could not have been any thicker. "We could see absolutely nothing of the enemy, nor any other part of our own lines," Major Robert Stiles, a Confederate soldier, would later lament. "Indeed, the entire region was a gloomy thicket and our infantry line so stretched and attenuated that the men were scarcely in sight of each other."[1] The Union side wasn't faring any better in what would become known as the Battle of Chancellorsville in Virginia. "We could not see what was going around us for the brush," stated Private David Holt of the Sixteenth Mississippi. "The fighting was hot and close ... because of the thick underbrush."[2]

The 24-year-old Major Barry did not see much of what was ahead of him—literally and figuratively speaking. Together with the Twenty-eighth North Carolina regiment and the Fiftieth Virginia, Barry's Eighteenth North Carolina was the outmost northeast extension of the Confederate line near the end of Bullock Road. A short distance away were three groups of men converging on one another, with dire consequences.

A Confederate general rode in with his closest confidants to inspect the line and plan his next move. Like in a giant maze, he was barely heard by his counterpart, a Union general doing the same thing just a couple hundred yards away. Between them, a lone horseman of the lost federal infantry unit, the 128th Pennsylvania, was about to ride directly into the main Confederate line.

Instantaneous rifle fire greeted the lost Union infantryman as he emerged from the thicket onto Bullock Road. The startled troops of the Confederate gray continued their volley blindly into the woods, long after the soldier had fallen. Like a giant wave, the musket fire spread down the entire Confederate line. The blind thundering of rifles tore into the Union general's scouting party, killing or wounding all but him alone. Further down the line, the rifle fire reached his Confederate counterpart. "Halt, who goes there?" shouted a young Confederate soldier as his shaking hands barely held on to his long rifle. The reply did not penetrate the bellowing noise around them. "Cease firing! You are firing into your own men!" yelled Lieutenant G. Morrison, a brother-in-law and staff member of the Confederate general he was now attempting to shield.[3] Major John Decatur Barry, the commanding officer of the Eighteenth North Carolina regiment, did not give the reply much chance of success. He ordered his men to fire. The shaky young man standing near Barry, like the hundreds of his brothers-in-arms around him, steadied his nerves and pulled the trigger.

Three bullets flew towards the mounted general. One found its mark in the palm of the man's right hand, one struck his lower left arm, and the third, most dangerous of all, lodged itself in his upper left arm, shattering a bone.[4] The general was roughly 90 yards away from the line of fire—a range in which a smoothbore musket has about a 1-in-16 chance of hitting its target when the shooter has a clear range of fire.[5] Yet this was not a firing range, it was a volley of blind fire into a dark and thick forest. As the weapons took just under a minute to load, and it was reported that the three bullets that met their mark did so simultaneously, it is clear that the general was downed by three separate soldiers. To this day we do not know which of the hundreds of North Carolinians fired the first shot—or the second or the third. There is no doubt, however, that the bullet that lodged itself in Confederate General Thomas "Stonewall" Jackson's shoulder the evening of May 2, 1863, would alter the fate of a nation.

* * * * * *

The year 1863, which was to decide the fate of the fledgling Confederate States of America and its more established neighbor, opened gloomily for both sides. The Confederate forces had failed to secure Maryland or win back any western lands lost to the United States. The South's great hope of being recognized by England and France was also fading, as was its food supply, stifled by the naval blockade of its ports. Its stockpiles of clothing, ammunition, and raw materials needed to wage war were all but depleted. The rebel nation was also unable to raise sufficient war funds by taxation or loans. The Confederacy had resorted to printing hundreds of millions of dollars of paper money, all but decimating its value. By the end of the war in 1865, it took a thousand Confederate dollars to buy a barrel of flour and $400 to buy a pair of shoes.[6]

Still, they were not the only ones not faring well. The great resources of the North could not save it from the great feeling of malaise that befell its people. The news coming from the front could not have been any more discouraging. Each day, narratives of defeat after defeat graced the front pages of city newspapers. Lincoln had finally pulled the plug on the slow-moving McClellan. He replaced him with General Ambrose E. Burnside, only to have the latter meet a terrible defeat in the reckless attack on Confederate General Robert E. Lee's impregnable position on Marye's Heights, near Fredericksburg, Virginia. This in turn resulted in Burnside being sidelined in favor of Joseph "Fighting Joe" Hooker who would go on to face—and lose—to the great military duo of General Lee and his right-hand man, General Thomas "Stonewall" Jackson, at the Battle of Chancellorsville. In fact, two years into the war, President Lincoln was still looking to find the right match for the famous Confederate generals.

It sure seemed that the only hope left for the Southerners was the tandem of Lee and Jackson continuing to elude their Union counterparts. By 1863, there were not many Southerners who deluded themselves with thoughts of a great military victory over the Union. The only chance left to the faltering nation was the continued success of its generals, their ability to inflict enough damage to the U.S. to push the already precarious political and social situation up North past its boiling point. The mounting taxes, together with the ever-growing casualty lists and repeated defeats, had more than cooled any support for the war and the nation's leadership. The voluntary enlistments fell to their lowest in their entire conflict in March of 1863. The leadership's answer in the form of the draft quickly escalated into riots across the North's major cities. When approximately a thousand people were killed in the government's attempt to suppress the draft riots, Congressman Clement L. Vallandigham, a war opponent from Ohio, declared publicly: "You have not conquered the South; you never will. The war with the Union ... is a bloody and costly failure. Money you have expended without limit, and blood poured out like water. Defeat, debt, taxation and sepulchers—these are your only trophies."[7] After the Democrats carried the important states of New York, Ohio, Indiana, Wisconsin, Illinois, and Pennsylvania and gained 32 seats in the House of Representatives, the writing was on the wall for President Lincoln. He needed victories, and he needed them fast.

The Battle of Chancellorsville took place on the heels of the Battle of Fredericksburg, one of the most one-sided battles of the entire Civil War. Fought between December 11 and 13, 1862, in Fredericksburg, Virginia, the battle revealed that the Union Army of the Potomac under General Ambrose Burnside was no match for the Confederate Army of Northern Virginia commanded by General Robert E. Lee and his right-hand man and cavalry officer Stonewall Jackson. When, on December 13, Burnside sent half of his strength—65,000 men—against Stonewall Jackson's 37,000 Confederates in a last-ditch attempt to turn the battle, his men fought their way into the heart of Stonewall's defenses only to be repelled by the never-give-up attitude of the Confederate general and his men.[8] The Union would go on to suffer nearly 13,000 casualties, more than double the number of men lost by its Southern counterpart. Major Burnside would quickly become another footnote in the parade of Union generals to command the Army of the Potomac.

Even before the Battle of Chancellorsville, where he would see his ultimate end, the legend of Thomas "Stonewall" Jackson was already deeply entrenched in Confederate lore. As the officer who never gave up, Jackson gained his nickname at the First Battle of Bull Run in July of 1861, where he charged his men against a Union attack. Confederate General Barnard E. Bee immortalized Jackson on that day, exclaiming, "There is Jackson standing like a stone wall!"[9] Following the battle, Thomas Jackson, henceforth referred to as "Stonewall Jackson," earned a promotion to major general.

By the spring of 1862, Jackson launched the Shenandoah Valley campaign, where, through his defense of western Virginia against American invaders, he solidified himself as one of the ablest commanders of the Confederate States of America. With an army of some 15,000 to 18,000 troops, Jackson repeatedly outmaneuvered a Union force of more than 60,000 men.[10] In fact, his troop movements were so fast that they would soon become known as the South's "foot cavalry." With the Union forces divided, Stonewall used his army's quickness to move from position to position and attack his enemy in such a confusing manner that he continuously claimed victories against larger yet often bewildered Union forces. By the campaign's conclusion, Thomas "Stonewall" Jackson had not only become the first Southern hero of the war and the Confederacy's greatest hope but also garnered the attention and admiration of both American and Confederate generals. Jackson's ability to thwart the Union's plans of sacking Richmond, Virginia, saw him promoted to join Lee's army in June of 1862.

The great partnership did not disappoint; in fact, Jackson's growing popularity and status as the most legendary commander of the Southern forces helped raise Robert E. Lee's stock with the Southern people. After joining the more senior general in June, Jackson's tactical prowess and bravery in battle saw him further distinguish himself as a pivotal part of the Southern strategy at the Second Battle of Bull Run and the Battle of Antietam—where his forces held their position until being recalled by Lee—and the Battle of Fredericksburg. By that time, Stonewall was Lee's main lieutenant general commanding a large portion of Lee's army. But the best was yet to come. With the exploits of generals such as Jackson and Lee, concurrent with the terribly worsening situation in the North, the Southern people had no doubts that their Confederate armies could press the U.S. just enough to bring them to the peace table and end hostilities between the two nations. The newest election results seeing Democrats and Copperheads (Republicans favoring the end of the war) gain seats in Congress signaled that the time was right.

Lee and Jackson's biggest victory, which in retrospect would prove to be more infamous than famous, took place in Virginia in 1863 near a crossroads in Chancellorsville, Virginia. The battle saw the Confederate army of 60,000 routing a numerically superior Union force of 130,000.[11] Splitting his army, Lee sent his most trusted general, Jackson, to attack the Union General Joseph Hooker's defensive position from the rear. In what is often considered Lee's finest moment, the success of the Confederate general could in fact be entirely attributed to the genius of Stonewall Jackson. Taking 28,000 of his troops and stealthily and quickly marching them undiscovered for 15 miles to Hooker's exposed flank, Jackson surprised the Union general, who thought he was facing the entire Confederate force on his front.[12] In reality, Lee's frontal assault was a diversion, while it was Jackson who would land the decisive blow. The Southern general's attack caused casualties in numbers that Hooker could not justify for any prolonged duration of time. The Union army was forced to withdraw just two days later. Upon hearing of Hooker's retreat, President Lincoln exclaimed, "My God! My God! What will the country say?"[13] Perhaps this new victory would be enough to force the North to negotiate a stalemate. Perhaps.

The attack of May 2, 1863, lasted all day. And although history now shows us that Hooker was already planning his inevitable retreat from Chancellorsville, Lee and Jackson did not yet know that was the case. As the sun set, Jackson ordered a small group of men to follow him into the dark forest to scout ahead. The most celebrated Confederate general of his time would leave the woods that night with three bullets in his body. His wounds would kill him within a week.

* * * * * *

It was perhaps the biggest blunder of Stonewall Jackson's military career. He wholeheartedly rode into terribly defined battle lines and into the darkest of dark forests full of tired soldiers who had just fought one of the biggest battles of their lives. His decision on the night of May 2, 1863, set into motion events that led not only to his own demise but likely the death of any chance that the Confederacy had of maintaining its existence.

It was a little after 9:00 p.m. when General Thomas "Stonewall" Jackson convinced his staff members to ride forward to the still disorganized Confederate line to assess the situation and make plans for the next day. Among those riding with the general was Captain Richard Eggleston Wilbourn, who would put pen to paper days later to describe the events of that night. As gunfire began randomly raining on them from the trees, the horses startled and moved the small company about 15 or so paces to the left of the road they were traveling on. Unfortunately, it placed them directly in front of another group of soldiers, who startled, promptly opened fire and striking Jackson. "The troops that fired at us did not appear to be more than thirty yards off, as I could see them thought it was after 9 o'clock p.m.," stated Wilbourn. "[Jackson] held his reins in his left hand [which was struck three times] which immediately dropped by his side and his horse perfectly frantic dashed back into the road, passing under the limb of a tree which took off his cap, and ran down the road towards the enemy."[14]

When Wilbourn and another man stopped Jackson's horse, they

all realized that, just as quickly as the firing ensued, it had now completely stopped. The young Wilbourn exclaimed that the shots had to have come from their own troops. Breathing heavily, the wounded general looked at him and nodded. Not much else needed to be said; they all knew what had happened. The biggest concern now was getting out of there alive. The men knew that they could not ride forward without risking capture, nor could they ride back the direction they'd come as it could unleash more friendly fire. After examining the general, Wilbourn assessed that Jackson, who was already leaning in his saddle, was looking none the better as blood continued to stream down his arm. Stonewall could stay up no longer. He fell into Wilbourn's arms. His feet, still in his stirrups, had to be removed by Mr. Wynn, another member of the group. "We laid him down on his back under a little tree with his head resting on my right leg for a pillow and proceeded to cut open his sleeve with my knife. I sent Mr. Wynn at once for Dr. [Hunter] McGuire and an ambulance as soon as I ripped up the India rubber ... he said, 'that's all right, cut away everything' ... [and added] 'It is providential [that we escaped alive].'"

The general managed to walk supported to friendly lines—at least the one section that realized what had just occurred and reined in their predisposition to shoot at anything that came their way. Unfortunately, that was not the case for the rest of the Confederate line. After being placed on a stretcher and carried through the woods to the rear of the line, the party was once again shot at. A bullet struck the stretcher-bearer, who promptly dropped his edge of the gurney. Jackson fell chest first into a rock, which briefly knocked him out. Upon reaching Doctor McGuire, the general was given first aid, which consisted of arterial compression, whiskey, and morphine.[15] He was then placed in a horse-drawn ambulance and transported to a field hospital.

The 26-year-old doctor quickly surmised that the need for surgery was urgent; the general's cold hands, clammy skin, and pale skin and lips pointed to hemorrhagic shock, he concluded. After learning of the doctor's order to have the left arm amputated, Jackson responded with a stoic, "Yes, certainly Dr. McGuire, do for me whatever you think best."[16] After the general was sedated with chloroform, McGuire began the procedure by extracting the round ball from his patient's right hand. Next, the good doctor later recalled, "the left arm was then amputated, about two inches below the shoulder, very rapidly, and with slight loss

---

of blood, the ordinary circular operation having been made."[17] For the time being all seemed to have gone well.

The next morning an aide arrived with a letter from General Robert E. Lee. "I have just received [a] note, informing me that you were wounded," Lee stated. "Could I have directed events I should have chosen for the good of the country to have been disabled in your stead." In return Stonewall dictated a message to his commander: "Better that ten Jacksons should fall than one Lee."[18] The heartwarming written exchange lasted for a couple of days as Lee sent over more letters: "You are better off than I am; for, while you have only lost your left, I have lost my right arm." The men did not yet know that the great Stonewall Jackson had only days to live.

The downfall of the great general began shortly after Jackson was moved to the Chandler plantation in the rural community of Guiney's Station, Virginia. The move was motivated by the need to rest as well as to keep the wounded general further away from the front lines. The plantation already contained other wounded Confederates and was serving as a makeshift hospital. Once there, Stonewall was met by his wife and baby daughter, who arrived shortly after him on May 7, 1863. Unfortunately, Mary Anna came just in time to see her husband's health turn for the worse. Jackson was suffering from pneumonia in his right lung. Questioned by Jackson's wife as to an explanation for such a sudden turn of events, Dr. McGuire attributed the sickness to the fall the general suffered while being carried away from the woods after being shot. "Contusion of the lung, with extravasation of blood in his chest, was probably produced by the fall referred to, and shock and loss of blood prevented any ill effects until reaction had been established, and then inflammation ensued," he commented.[19] Still, in later years and with more modern scientific and medical research, doctors now believe that a bacterial infection stemming from his amputated arm traveled to his lungs, all but ensuring Jackson's eventual death.[20]

On the night of May 10, 1863, with his consciousness fading and his wife near his side, Jackson opened his eyes one last time and cried out in confusion, "Order A.P. Hill to prepare for action! Pass the infantry to the front rapidly! Tell Major Hawks...." The sentence was never finished. He then turned towards his wife, his eyes closing, and, this time in a more subtle voice, spoke his final words, "Let us pass over the river, and rest under the shade of the trees."[21] After a few more inspirations, his

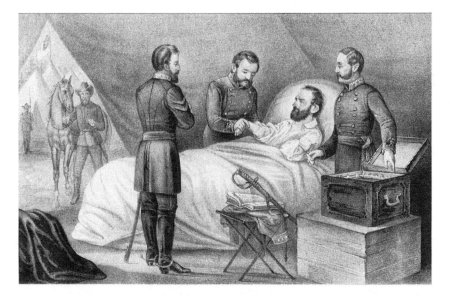

The lithograph depicts the death of Thomas "Stonewall" Jackson. By the time of this death, the general had already suffered the amputation of his left arm, something that would lead General Robert E. Lee to proclaim, "[Jackson] lost his left arm, but I have lost my right" (Currier & Ives, Library of Congress).

breath ceased. With it the hope for the people of the South, who were still clinging to the idea of some sort of Confederate victory.

* * * * * *

When looking at the biggest turning points of the Civil War, while the death of Thomas "Stonewall" Jackson was perhaps not on par with the fall of Vicksburg or Lee's defeat at Gettysburg, it most certainly was a setback that the Confederacy could ill afford in 1863. Apart from dealing a massive blow to morale, the event stifled any momentum the South had heading into the second half of the year, especially after the victories at Fredericksburg and Chancellorsville. It would be equally inane to ignore the role that Stonewall played in both of those victories. Battles that only added to the already dire social and political situation in the North, which needed to be exploited. Unfortunately for the South— and fortunately for the nation's history as a whole—the next few months would see a culmination of events that would reverse the war's narrative in the Union's favor. General Robert E. Lee's invasion of the North and the subsequent Battle of Gettysburg, where the Confederacy glaringly missed their brilliant tactician Thomas "Stonewall" Jackson, turned the tide in the North's favor far enough where there was no longer any doubt where the war was headed. Concurrent with the Union's victory at Vicksburg and the ascendance of Union General Ulysses S. Grant, the South would never again threaten its Northern adversary. For the Confederacy, 1863 was a year of two halves, one dominated by victories spearheaded by the exceptionally talented tandem of Robert E. Lee and Thomas "Stonewall" Jackson and one where the partnership was prematurely cut short and the Confederate dream permanently derailed.

The most immediate effect of Jackson's death was witnessed through the great dirge that spread across the South. Thousands turned out to see their fallen hero as the general's body lay in state at the capitol in Richmond, Virginia. All this paled in comparison to the numbers of mourners that greeted the train that moved the deceased to Lynchburg for the last procession before being moved to its final resting place in Lexington. It all seemed so dreamlike. So unbelievable. The news of Stonewall's death came as a shock that echoed across the South. As his body was being transferred across town by a horse-drawn carriage that would bring it to the canal and the packet boat for its voyage to Lexington, people turned out en masse. Businesses were ordered shut, church bells serenaded the procession, and the thunder of small cannons fired in respect reverberated across the town. *The Daily Virginian* proclaimed: "The greatest thunderbolt of the war has perished.... He stood peerless and alone ... in face of vigor, and celerity of his movements, he was Napoleonic ... nor has there been a campaign equal to that brief and brilliant [fight] which cleared the Shenandoah Valley of the enemy, since the day Napoleon swept like a comet over Italy... [Jackson] gave his life in defense of the altars and fire-sides of his people and in vindication of the sacred principle of liberty."[22]

It was dark when the procession finally reached the banks of the canal, and the body was loaded for the overnight trip to its final destination. To those present in Lynchburg on that day, it seemed like the setting sun had a deeper meaning. The darkness, which now draped the coffin of the fallen leader being loaded on a barge, was the end of a chapter in the short history of a hopeful nation. When the sun came up the next morning, the situation between the two nations, as much as it seemed unchanged, would in fact never be the same. The great victories of the recent year were attributed to the South's two great generals, Lee and Jackson—a collaboration now broken forever. How would the destruction of this partnership affect the Confederacy's momentum? On March 14, 1864, no one knew the answer. But they would soon find out.

General Robert E. Lee was eager to stifle the spread of the quiet unease reverberating across his army after the news of Jackson's death. After all, he and Jackson had just won a most dazzling victory at the Battle of Chancellorsville. It was now time to press the initiative and launch the boldest strike of the war. Without his right-hand man, who had so many times come to his rescue just when the battle seemed lost, Lee crossed the Potomac River on June 15, 1863, with an army of 70,000, seeking the great victory that would terrorize Washington, close the vaults of the Northern bankers financing the war, and wreck the sorely tired government of Lincoln.[23] The meeting between his Army of Northern Virginia and Union General George Meade's army of 8,000 would make a little Pennsylvania town of Gettysburg infamous for staging the greatest battle of the entire Civil War. The subsequent Confederate loss in July of 1863 would subsequently begin the ultimate end of the Confederacy and the end of slavery in the United States, all while setting the nation up on a path towards eventual reunification.

The Battle of Gettysburg is one of the greatest what-ifs in American history. What if Lee had still had Jackson? The death of his greatest general forced Lee to reorganize the strategy and fighting force that was responsible for his two greatest victories at Fredericksburg and Chancellorsville. To compensate for the lack of Jackson's tactical prowess, the Army of Northern Virginia changed its two-corps structure into three corps under James Longstreet, Ambrose P. Hill, and Richard Ewell.[24] In this new configuration, Lee did not have to promote anyone to assume Jackson's place—for which he believed he did not have a worthy successor. This made the army units smaller and thus easier to command by his three new generals. And while there is no way of telling how different Gettysburg would have turned out with Stonewall Jackson alive, we can definitely assume that Lee would have kept his army's proven and previously victorious two-corps structure, undoubtedly changing the Confederate general's orders during those three fateful days in Pennsylvania.

As it stands, the defeat at Gettysburg cost the South much of its already hindered fighting power. Low on ammunition, not to mention food or basic necessities such as clothing and shoes, the army was no longer able to wage offensive warfare. Its hope of holding on just long enough to destroy the dwindling Northern morale and instigate a cease-fire had faded. The victory also proved to be the North's morale booster, one that the South itself hoped for. As Southern newspapers began calling for an end to all hostilities, the United States had finally found itself a general worthy of Lee. Just a few weeks after Gettysburg, Union General Ulysses S. Grant would be promoted to oversee the U.S. military effort. Not unlike Thomas "Stonewall" Jackson, Grant's assertive nature and go-get-it attitude would see him triumph over his foes and steer the war to its end.

But what if Jackson never chose to ride out that night in Chancellorsville? What if he lived to lead his victorious troops once more at Gettysburg? Following the train of thought that sees Jackson surviving and leading one of Lee's two corps at Gettysburg, the biggest emphasis falls on the performance of General Richard Ewell, whose forces Jackson would have commanded. It just so happens that it is Ewell's failure on the first day of the battle that historians point to as the catalyst for the eventual loss. It is assumed that all of Stonewall Jackson's past actions, characterized by swift initiative and persistence, would have found the assault on Cemetery Hill feasible. The outcome of which would have given the Confederate forces the upper hand in the battle and set the tone for its remaining days. Ewell chose to second-guess his ability to seize the battle position and made the prudent decision to not do so. The Battle of Fredericksburg had shown that Jackson's predisposition to aggressiveness in battle had made him push forward, even when the situation did not look favorable. It is thus believed that, had he lived, Jackson would have commanded a much larger force than Ewell's one third of the Army of Northern Virginia and, using his tendency to press forward against questionable odds, would have seized the important military positions at Gettysburg. The rest, as they say, would have been history. Yet, as things stand, we have to settle on this narrative simply being one of the greatest what-ifs in the annals of American history.

FOR FURTHER READING

If one wants to review one of the earliest accounts of Stonewall Jackson's military campaigns and his death, the best place to begin would be Professor R.L. Dabney's *Life and Campaign of Lieut.-Gen. Thomas J. Jackson* (1866). It is a very glorifying and unapologetic portrait of the Southern general that does not yet benefit from historical perspective that often accompanies research conducted years after the event being described. For a more modern re-telling of Jackson's contribution to the Southern effort and the significance of his death, one needs not look any further than Pulitzer Prize finalist writer S.C. Gwynne's *Rebel Yell: The Violence, Passion, and Redemption of Stonewall Jackson* (2014). Of interest might be Richard E. Beringer's book *Why the South Lost the Civil War* (1986). It does not specifically account for Jackson's death as a contribution to the Confederacy's downfall but does delve into the losses suffered by General Lee in the years following Stonewall's death. Along the same lines is *Why the North Won the Civil War* (1996) by two-time Pulitzer Prize winner David Herbert Donald, which contains six authoritative views on the reasons for the South's demise. Last but not least, the more recent *The Great Partnership: Robert E. Lee, Stonewall Jackson, and the Fate of the Confederacy* (2019) by Christian B. Keller outlines the important role Jackson played in Lee's Army of Northern Virginia.

6

A "Square" Fight, May 3, 1886

Initially tasked with overseeing the peaceful end to a workday at the McCormick Reaper Works, Chicago police officer William O'Brien found himself dead center in a commotion that was quickly turning into a riot. Stationed outside the plant, he hurried towards the gates to join the rest of the police force that had just arrived at McCormick's. He never made it. As the number of rioters grew around him, slowing down his pace, the young officer was struck on the face by a large rock—and then another. A split second after discharging his weapon towards the aggressors, O'Brien's bullet hit a man named August Neukopf, who instantly fell to the ground. With blood pouring from his forehead, the officer continued towards the McCormick Reaper Works. Fifty yards away, the body of the fallen man was quickly taken away by fellow dissidents.

By the end of the day, four men would lie dead. Apart from O'Brien's bullet, his fellow police officers shot three more men in their feeble attempt to contain the mayhem of the striking mob attacking strikebreakers leaving the McCormick factory. Within 24 hours, outrage at the police brutality of that day prompted a rally in nearby Haymarket Square to protest the four killings. The subsequent bomb explosion and the panicked police shots fired into the crowd on that day would alter the public's perception of unions and, more importantly, set the labor movement back for years to come.

* * * * *

The conflict between capital and organized labor grew to such a large extent by the middle of the 1880s that contemporaries began referring to it as the time of "the great upheaval." Strikes increased from 485 in 1884 to 645 in 1885 and 1411 in 1886—the year of the McCormick uprising and the Haymarket Square riot—and by the following year would involve nearly 10,000 establishments and a half a million workers.[1] In the greater context, the basis for reforms—commonly known to historians as the revolt against rugged individualism—evolved from the desolate political turmoil that followed the Civil War. The responsibility for the change could be attributed to workers and farmers who were jaded by big business and a new belief in government involvement in righting the nation's wrongs. If railroad rates were too high, they argued, the government should protect shippers by forcing the railroads to lower their charges; if a business became so monopolistic that it could charge unreasonable prices, it should be broken down into competing units.[2] This was in contrast to the long-standing belief of laissez-faire capitalism, where private and corporate affairs were free of any government interference. The second industrial revolution, which followed the Civil War, changed all of that.

As far as a working-class American was concerned, the biggest drawback of post-war industrialization was the shift from skilled craftsmanship to simple factory work. For a common worker, the most significant consequences stemming from this paradigm shift included the loss of bargaining power that his skills and tools had previously given him; the impersonality of employer-employee relations in the new corporations; and increased competition for jobs resulting from the entry into the labor force of former slaves, women, and immigrants.[3] All of this was on top of the more common long hours, the meager weekly wages, and the appallingly unhealthy and dangerous working conditions in factories.

It is not surprising that as much as their fates are connected, employers and employees have very divergent goals. While the former strives to achieve efficiency in acquiring the greatest profits possible from their business and labor, the latter looks for any means of improving their status in the workplace. In late 1800, this meant organizing effectively. There were essentially three primary aims of organized labor during the McCormick uprising and the Haymarket Square riot in Chicago: higher wages, reduced hours, and safer working conditions. As fighting tools, the newly organized national unions utilized strikes, boycotts, and simple picketing.

The situation in 1880 was quite dire for working-class Americans.

6. A "Square" Fight, May 3, 1886

The rise of big corporations had all but ended any personal relationship between management and labor as companies were now governed by members of elected boards of directors instead of direct business owners. Without that personal touch, the workers felt they needed to look elsewhere for support as having a good relationship with one's boss was no longer probable. Further compounding the problem was the mechanization of industry, which diminished the reliance on skilled artisans and sought unskilled labor now easily supplied by immigration. As living costs increased, wages remained steady at around $10 and $20 a week for unskilled and skilled work, respectively. As a result, many wives and children were forced to also enter the workforce. The average worker logged between 10 and 12 hours a day, excluding Sundays when workers often received their day off. For context: in 1899, women earned an average of $267 a year, half as much as their male counterparts—in contrast, Andrew Carnegie that same year made $23 million with no income tax laws in place.[4] As for the factories that employed the young and the old, the male and the female alike, they were badly ventilated and dark and hazardous thanks to unmonitored machinery. In 1882 an average of 675 laborers were killed in work-related accidents each week.[5]

There were ultimately three stages of organization that followed the Civil War. First came the National Labor Union. Established in 1866 through merging local craft unions and reform groups, this union extended organizing into the national realm through a publicity campaign. Yet, perhaps the most successful organization to strive for the betterment of labor during the McCormick riot was the Knights of Labor. Formed in 1869, the Knights attempted to unite workers of all skill, color, and creed into "One Big Union" that could wrestle from employers a more equitable share of the nation's wealth.[6] The organization won its first grand victory in 1884 when a strike on the Missouri Pacific Railroad led to the reinstatement of wages after an attempt was made by management to cut them. The local unions finally had a prestigious big brother they could look to for support in their struggle for better working conditions. By the beginning of 1886, the Knights of Labor had more than 700,000 members. Additionally, more than 100 local political tickets across the nation were associated with the organization between 1886 and 1888, from Anniston, Alabama, to Whitewater, Wisconsin, aimed at ending the use of public and private police forces and court injunctions against strikes and labor organizations.[7]

Bullets That Changed America

As membership in national unions grew, so did its "Big Business" opposition. And as it happens, those in power in the nation's economic sector were also holding the reins in the political one. In fact, one would be hard-pressed to see the government side with the unions in labor disputes prior to the 1900s. Most notably, the corporations sought and received federal aid in their quest to subdue union actions. Companies had to report to the federal government that a strike or a boycott—or even a picket line—was hurting interstate trade, and an injunction against the union soon followed. While these legal hurdles imposed by the government lessened the effectiveness of unions, they did not compare to the day-to-day struggle against the business owners themselves.

The management did not recognize unions as true representatives of their workforce, and many factories disallowed organized meetings and even went as far as to fire those who joined them. By the mid–1880s, many companies forced new employees to sign "yellow dog contracts," which were oaths promising that the individual would never join a union. To further counter the growing power of organized labor, companies attempted to keep their workers in check by enacting lockouts. Viewed as the opposite of a strike, a company representative would set out before the start of a shift and greet a portion of the workforce by telling them that there was no work for them on that day. This would happen for a few days until the same manager would show up at the gate and proclaim that the workers could come back to work if they agreed to a pay cut or longer work hours. If the workers' union organized a strike in retaliation, the business would hire strikebreakers, more commonly known at the time as "scabs." These temporary and non-union workers, who were often poor recent immigrants, would take the place of the regular working force and show up for work thankful for the little pay they received. At this point, strikes would often turn violent as scabs trying to enter or leave the factory would be met by angry unionized workers whose jobs they were seen as stealing.

Although not endorsed by the nationally recognized union Knights of Labor, the smaller trade unions across the nation set May 1, 1886, as the unofficial deadline for being granted a standard eight-hour workday. With the date set, news spread like wildfire. Union members prepared for a national strike as the front pages of the nation's top newspapers warned against the anticipated riots. Ultimately, the workers did not disappoint, responding devotedly with demonstrations across the nation. As is often the case with any movement, organized events had to contend with radicals possessing abstract theories lacking any substantial practicality of action. These more intense proponents of a total reorganization of the social order, referred to as "anarchists," denounced corporations' vast, state-supported power and often displayed their anti-capitalist views by inciting violence against those in power. And while neither the union labor movement nor the Knights of Labor considered themselves anarchists, this did not stop some more radical union members across the nation from associating themselves with the concurring revolutionaries.

By the 1880s, Chicago, fueled by a large German and generally European population, became the hotbed of anarchism. The immigrants had arrived on the shores of the United States, having spent their lives under many totalitarian governments, and learned to reject what they saw as an involuntary and forced form of power or even social hierarchy. These individuals would interpret any abuse of authority as a threat to their newly found freedoms. As such, for many, the plight of the labor class became synonymous with the anarchist message. In the city of Chicago, where anarchist leaders were of the syndicalist nature and favored violence to counter capitalist subjugation, individuals went as far as hosting the 1881 Congress of the Black International [International Working People's Association].[8] The meeting would unite anarchist delegates from as many as 14 cities across the nation. It would bring together individuals who would later be prosecuted for the Haymarket bombings, which were indirectly caused by the McCormick riot of 1886.

In 1885, the year before the McCormick riot, the iron molders union organized a strike at the plant in response to having their wages reduced by the company known for producing agricultural machinery. After McCormick brought in scabs to replace the picketing workers and utilized a privatized police force to protect them against the strikers, the ensuing battles prompted the corporation to give in to the strikers' demands. Yet, that would not be the case in 1886, when innovative machinery installed at the plant reduced the need for the very same artisans who had won a great victory just a year prior. Fueled by the national deadline for securing an eight-hour workday, the already striking citizens of Chicago, including many from the agricultural plant, gathered in the city's industrial center. Then the bell signaling the end of a workday rang. As the strikebreakers hired by the McCormick corporation waited for the big gates to open and let them out, thousands of angry rioters, fueled by the loud voices of select anarchists dispersed amongst them, awaited them on the other side. The riot that ensued would see four men lose their lives and spark a bigger riot at Haymarket Square, which would not only set the labor movement back but forever taint the public perception of union actions by associating them with extreme radicalism.

* * * * * *

The *Chicago Tribune* of May 4, 1886, began its 10-page edition with the following words in what it called the "first serious outbreak of the labor troubles":

A Wild Mob's Work. Ten Thousand Men Storm McCormick's Harvester Works. Wrought Up to a Frenzy by Anarchistic Harangues They Attack the Employers as They Come from Work—Two Hundred Police Charge the Rabble and Use Their Revolvers—Rioters and Policemen Wounded—Arrests Made—An Inflammatory Circular....[9]

The account of the event was deconstructed throughout the entire first page of the paper, with many editorials condemning it throughout the latter pages. In fact, the reporters who found themselves among the mob managed to write just enough of what transpired in their notepads before they themselves were found out and severely beaten. The city did not yet know that the events on that Monday, May 3, were just a harbinger for the real newsworthy event that would dominate their papers for weeks to come.

It was three o'clock when men began to assemble at the predetermined spot on the prairie that stood out among the industrial lumber district of Chicago. Many of those who arrived had done so after visiting local pubs and spending their last money drinking away their sorrows. May 3 was like any other early summer day, sunny and mildly warm. Looking around, one could easily have estimated the turnout to be anywhere between 6,000 and 7,000 rioters. There were several freight cars standing on the railroad tracks about 100 yards from the McCormick plant, from which speakers addressed the ever-growing assembly of disgruntled workers. The *Chicago Tribune* reported that "in this part of the city, the Anarchistic element outnumber[ed] the peaceable ones twenty to one." Adding that "they were all there," the *Tribune* further noted that several hundred people in the crowd "cheered every inflammatory utterance."[10]

As Fritz Schmidt, a Socialist from the Central Labor Union, got atop of one of the freight cars and promptly ripped off his jacket, the crowd—many members of which had had a bit too much to drink that morning—erupted in cheers. "On to McCormick's," he screamed, "and let us run every one of the damned scabs out of the city!" Schmidt continued as the crowd below him erupted in cheers. "It is they who are taking the bread from you, your wives, and your children. On to them!" His voice was booming. "Blow up the factory! Strike for your freedom, and if the armed murderers of law interfere, shoot them down as you would the scabs!" The man paused dramatically and finished his oratory. "Revolution is the only remedy. Do not be afraid! Arm yourselves! ... Be men ... and get what rightfully belongs to you!" The crowd began to chant, "On to McCormick's!"[11]

The men within the factory who accepted the company's terms of reduced personnel with longer hours nervously awaited the bell that would signal their dismissal for the day. When the bell finally sounded off, the dissidents ran towards the factory. The gates opened, and men poured out. Only about 100 could make it before the approaching mob barricaded their way and pelted the strikebreakers with stones. As officer William O'Brien was getting caught in the mob outside the plant, one lone officer, Lt. West, was guarding the gate only to be chased off by a large man wielding a knife. The remaining 700 workers who were unable to leave retreated into the grounds of the McCormick plant, unfortunately not fast enough to secure the big gate behind them. Making their way through the retreating scabs, armed guards ran towards the mob and promptly discharged their guns into the air to dissuade the oncoming rioters. As loose bricks and crowbars flew towards them, the helpless security retreated. By now, the mob had broken down the gate and was pouring into the courtyard and towards the terrified workers.

O'Brien could see the Hinman Street patrol wagon loaded with police reinforcements cutting through the mob as he was instinctively reaching for his weapon to fire the first of four fatal shots to be discharged that day. As the wagon dashed towards the gate with the horses urged into a mad gallop, hundreds of voices could be heard screaming, "Kill the police!"[12] Dodging bricks, stones, and clubs, the police officers drew the wagon before the gate and jumped off, guns in hand. With the revolvers leveled at them, the crowd waivered, albeit only momentarily. Busy avoiding stones hurled in their direction, the officers panicked when the crowd started chanting, "Shoot them!" Then, as if scripted, members of the rioters pulled out guns and began shooting towards the 12 armed policemen who by then were pushed into the factory's courtyard. While none of the shots proved to be fatal, the same could not be said for the retaliating bullets coming from the police. Identified as a "stray bullet" by the *Chicago Chronicle*, one projectile struck the foremost man in the crowd. Hit in the groin, the 23-year-old Joseph Vojtik would be the second fatality that day. Two more men would be shot and confirmed killed within an hour—some early accounts had the number at six. The identities of the four were never confirmed, as they were quickly whisked away from the shooting scene by other rioters to protect their families from possible repercussions.

The tense situation continued for nearly an hour, with gunshots fired in all directions. It was a miracle that there were only four deaths that day. Heads of tenants could be seen in every window, fearfully observing the mayhem below. It was later reported that many of those who sustained injuries were brought into those very same tenement houses to receive first aid. When the police later inquired about the men who needed the assistance, they received no cooperation from the tenants. Down below, a large man holding a club continued to taunt the police officers who kept on waving in and out from the cover of the wagon. Just when all hope seemed lost, and it appeared that the mob would overpower them, reinforcements in the shape of countless police wagons full of officers arrived at the scene.

Using clubs, the officers mercilessly smashed into the crowd, which at first attempted to hold the ground. "The crowd poured a shower of stones into the new arrivals, but the heroic [men] now advanced on the [rioters], and making a charge from both ends, the police struck at heads with clubs and pistols and arrested several whom they had spotted as leaders."[13] Within 30-odd minutes, it was all over. Afraid of being shot at and having seen the violence directed towards those deemed responsible for inciting them, the crowd began to disperse. "The prisoners were badly cut up and wounded and were kept in the yard until additional police arrived," upon which they were taken to the police station and charged with rioting.[14] With relative peace restored, the strikebreakers were placed in a line and escorted out of the factory under the strong guard of the police. As for the rioters themselves, while some still lingered, most of them scattered by fleeing in every possible direction. Many wound up safely hidden behind the doors of local citizens who also worked in the district and were distrustful of big business.

It was dark and eerily quiet on the streets of Chicago that evening. Police officers patrolled the now empty city streets when they came across pamphlets distributed over Chicago's West Side. Written in English on one side and German on the other, the circular imitated (the *Tribune* pointed out) the anonymous circulars that often preceded the outbreak of great revolutions of Europe. Signed "Your Brother," the leaflets intended to incite retaliation for recent police brutality.

> Your masters sent out their bloodhounds—the police; they killed six of your brothers at McCormick's this afternoon. They killed the poor wretches, because they, like you, had the courage to disobey the supreme will of your bosses. They killed them because they dared to ask for the shortening of the hours of toil. They killed them to show you, "Free American Citizens," that you must be satisfied and contented with whatever your bosses condescend to allow you, or you will get killed! ... If you are men, if you are the sons of your grand sires, who have shed their blood to free you, then you will rise in your might, Hercules, and destroy the hideous monster that seeks to destroy you. To arm we call you, to arms![15]

Concurrent with the circular, the anarchists called a protest meeting for the following evening at Haymarket Square. The intent was to hold a rally to bring awareness to the brutal and deadly police tactics against strikers at the McCormick Harvesting Machine Company plant. The meeting that stemmed directly from the events of the day prior, most notably from the killing of four men, which started with the bullet fired at August Neukopf by Officer William O'Brien, could not have gone any worse. The events that transpired that day all but relegated the McCormick incident that caused them to historical obscurity—or at most made it a simple footnote to the more significant event that came to be known as the Haymarket Square riot.

* * * * * *

The rally held at Haymarket Square on May 4, 1886, went smoother than anticipated by the local papers. And although those participating—1,500 or so persons—were, by all accounts, orderly, this did not prevent the city's mayor from ordering the police to march into the square just as the meeting ended. With the final speech just finishing, someone—whose identity has been lost to history forever—threw a bomb into the crowd, killing a policeman and wounding countless others. The panicked police officers unleashed a barrage of fire, frantically shooting and killing innocent bystanders and a number of their own.[16] Some rally participants pulled their own guns, and by the time the dust settled, seven police members lay dead, with at least 60 more in the crowd left wounded.[17]

News of the Haymarket riot caused national hysteria. The citizens' fear and rage were directed at anarchists and the labor unions they were now seen to command. In fact, the incident severely injured the labor movement by shifting the public opinion to associate all union action with violence. Soon enough, people's wrath spilled over past union leaders into strikers, immigrants, and even the working class as a whole. A total of eight anarchists were charged with organizing and executing the bombing. And although the evidence against them in the plot was spotty at best, the jury was quick to judge them. "Convict these men," exclaimed the state's attorney, Julius S. Grinnell, "make examples of them, hand them, and you save our institutions."[18] Out of the eight put on trial, four were hanged, one committed suicide once in prison, and the remaining three were imprisoned.

The historically forward-reaching repercussions of the events were set into motion almost immediately and were still felt nearly a hundred years later. Business went on the offensive. It now felt justified to use violence to break up strikes, blacklist strikers, and intensify the signing of yellow-dog contracts. Anarchism and the labor movement were now so entrenched together in people's minds that the membership in the Knights of Labor, perhaps the most successful union up to that point in American history, declined rapidly. Furthermore, the already shaky sentiment towards immigrants shifted towards more distrust and discrimination. By the time of the McCormick and Haymarket riots, the anarchist movement of Chicago was already known for forming the International Working People's Association in 1883, which openly advocated violence in the class struggle. And because the majority of the membership was recruited from the immigrant population, anarchism and immigration became intertwined. Of the eight anarchist newspapers published in Chicago at the time, only one was printed in English.[19] In the public eye, being an immigrant meant being an anarchist, which

6. A "Square" Fight, May 3, 1886

The anarchist riot at Haymarket Square in Chicago, where a dynamite bomb exploded among the police, was really started at the McCormick Harvesting Machine Company a couple of days prior. The two events would spell doom for the future of unionization in the U.S. (drawn by T. de Thulstrup from sketches and photographs furnished by H. Jeaneret, *Harper's Weekly* v. 30 [May 15, 1886], pp. 312–313, Library of Congress).

in turn meant being a rabble-rouser. After the Haymarket Square riot caused by the events at McCormick's, the labor union could be added to the mix.

Populist historian Howard Zinn would go on to write that while the immediate result of the McCormick and Haymarket Square riots "was the suppression of the radical movement, the long-term effect was to keep alive the class anger of many to inspire others—especially young people of that generation—to action in revolutionary causes."[20] In the months that followed the trial and sentencing of those deemed responsible for the Haymarket Square bombing, the governor of Illinois, John Peter Altgeld, was bombarded with thousands of signed petitions asking for clemency for the remaining three imprisoned men. After further investigations, the governor agreed that the evidence against them was insufficient to warrant the verdict. Three years after being found guilty of anarchism, the three men were pardoned and released. The same could not be said of four of their accomplices for whom the justice department was not as favorable. Zinn further pointed out: "Year after year, all over the county, memorial meetings for the Haymarket martyrs were held; it is impossible to know the number of individuals whose political awakening—as with Emma Goldman and Alexander Berkman, long-time revolutionary stalwarts of the next generation—came from the Haymarket Affair."[21]

* * * * * *

An explosion rocked a Chicago neighborhood just before midnight on a chilly October night. An eight-foot statue was blown off of its pedestal. The police statement identified the cause of the explosion as a dynamite stick that blew the legs off the figure and blew out at least 40 windows at a nearby office building. A picture in the paper showed a police officer standing near the scene and looking down on the plaque on the now-empty pedestal. It read: "Standing in memory of seven Chicago police officers martyred in the anarchist riots of May 4, 1886."[22] It was Monday, October 6, 1969. The Windy City was still trying to pick itself up from the violent clashes between the police and protesters two months prior at the National Democratic Convention. As the now toppled statue showed, for Chicago and the nation, the struggle between those in power and those who viewed themselves as oppressed by them was far from over.

For Further Reading

Henry David's *The History of the Haymarket Affair: A Study of the American Social-Revolutionary and Labor Movements* (1963) is a good start here. Yet it has been out of print for quite some time and may be difficult to get ahold of. More accessible and written in significantly more straightforward prose is James Green's *Death in the Haymarket: A Story of Chicago* (2006). There is also the History Press's publication of Joseph Anthony Rulli's *The Chicago Haymarket Affair* (2016), an investigation and moment-by-moment recounting of the Haymarket incident as well as the trial that followed. *A History of America in Ten Strikes* (2020) by Erik Loomis dedicates a whole chapter to the fight for reduced hours, and while it does not spend a lot of time on the Haymarket affair, it does a great job placing it in context. Last but most certainly not least are countless newspaper articles available online through various paid subscriptions such as newspapers.com and nytimes.com. The place to start with in relation to analyzing the primary sources of the event would have to be the *Chicago Tribune,* which covered all the events described in this chapter extensively during the labor unrests of 1886.

7

Black Coyote's Rifle,
December 29, 1890

A large group of men, women, and children of the Lakota nation sat in a large semicircle on the cold, snow-covered ground. It was around 8:00 a.m. on December 29, 1890, and the people, numbering in the hundreds, looked tired. Perhaps tired of being chased out of their land. Or tired of being hungry. Or tired of fighting. But all of that is just speculation.

Looking up, a young Native American could just make out the faces of the Seventh Cavalry troops filling out the ridges surrounding the camp—located near a bend of the Wounded Knee Creek. His eyes settled on the four Hotchkiss guns strategically placed on a ridge about 200 yards away. And then his glance returned to the man dressed in blue parading in front of the tribe.

Major Whiteside would later say that he did not want a fight. He ordered the Native American men to come up, 20 at a time, and give up their arms—hoping the show of force would be enough to deter any resistance. The first group of 20 came up, yet only three rifles were delivered. The next group came empty-handed. Whiteside was being pressured to make this hasty by his superior, General Forsyth, standing a few paces behind him. With the lack of cooperation from the Native Americans now evident, an order was given for those soldiers of the Seventh on foot to enter the teepees and search for any weapons. Those at the scene would later recall two things, the cold and tense situation among all present when the troops began their search and the equally extreme weather around them.

A medicine man, "gaudily dressed and fantastically painted," stood up and began chanting as he performed the Ghost Dance. As he spoke in his native tongue, Philip Wells, a mixed-blood Sioux and an army interpreter struggled to keep up with the English translation. Nearly screaming over the loud Lakota, Wells exclaimed simultaneously, "I have lived long enough." Turning towards the young Native American men sitting down, the old man's voice thundered behind Wells's translation: "Do not fear, but let your hearts be strong! ... Their bullets cannot penetrate us!" The man paused and then pointed at Whiteside; the interpreter continued to translate: "If they [bullets] do come toward us, they will float away like dust in the air."[1]

General Forsyth approached the circle and ordered Wells to tell the medicine man to stop screaming. Instead, the old man began making his way around the circle, chanting without pause. Annoyed, Forsyth ordered the Native Americans to remove their blankets and directed Troop "K" to search them for weapons. The medicine man, known to the tribe as Yellow Bird, was nearly done making his way around the circle when a soldier found a new Winchester rifle belonging to a young Miniconjou named Black Coyote.

Black Coyote raised the rifle above his head, shouting that he had paid a lot of money for the rifle, and it was rightfully his. The nearby soldiers shouted back at him to stop waving the weapon in the air. They did not understand him, nor did he understand them. The screams intensified. Yellow Bird finally made his way around the circle, only adding to the noise and commotion. Black Coyote did not hear his rifle go off as the bullet sprung up into the sky; nor did he hear the volley of weapons that ensued from the nearby American soldiers returning fire.

Black Coyote did not understand the soldiers' pleas that he put down his weapon. He could not even hear them. For Black Coyote was deaf. Now his fate—and those of 300 of his people—would be much worse, as would be those of thousands of Native Americans across the Great Plains.

* * * * * *

"The white children have surrounded me and have left me nothing but an island," proclaimed the great Sioux Chief Red Cloud in 1870, the year after the completion of the transcontinental railroad. "When we first had all this land, we were strong; now we are all melting like snow on a hillside, while you are grown like spring grass."[2] While the Native American tribes east of the Mississippi had been all but subdued or pushed west into Indian Territory (today Oklahoma), the nomadic nations of the Great Plains continued their struggle against western expansion all the way until the late nineteenth century. This struggle would culminate with the discharge of Black Coyote's rifle and the subsequent Wounded Knee massacre in South Dakota. As historian Kenneth C. Davis would say years later, Wounded Knee would prove to be the Indians' "last stand."[3]

Ever since Native Americans acquired horses brought over by the Spanish conquistadors in the late sixteenth century, they began to roam the grasslands extending throughout the central portion of the United States. This increased mobility often led to conflicts among the tribal nations, as whole tribes would encroach on already claimed hunting grounds. This would lead to the creation of war parties and a warrior-like identity that would prove fatal once it clashed with the westward expansion of the United States in the mid- to late-1800s. Another point of contention apart from the rights to hunting grounds was the discrepancy in the social norms of the Native Americans and the whites moving into their lands. Living in small extended family groups, with specifically defined gender roles—men as warriors and women as laborers preparing the hunted game for consumption or otherwise—the Native Americans also believed in powerful spirits controlling the world around them. Subsequently, unlike their white counterparts, the tribes did not believe in land ownership or claims. This made the creation of many treaties with the Americans that much easier, as apart from having hunting rights, the concept of land privatization was outside of Native American culture.

While Americans looked to hunting the buffalo as just another capitalist endeavor, to the various tribes of the Great Plains, the animal fulfilled their most basic needs and was central to their way of life. In fact, it was their source of clothing, shelter, fuel, and, most importantly, food. Apart from making teepees from buffalo hides and using the skins for clothing, shoes, and blankets, the animal's meat was dried into jerky or mixed with berries and fat to make a food staple called pemmican.[4] At the beginning of the nineteenth century, nearly 65 million buffalo roamed the plains; by the end of the decade, that number would dwindle to a mere 1000. It comes as no surprise that the tribes native to the West—especially the Cheyenne, Comanche, Crow, Kiowa, and Sioux— viewed the whites' expansion into western lands as a threat to their way of life. And nothing signified this better than fur traders, or even tourists, shooting the buffalo for sport. After the transcontinental railroad was built, it was not uncommon to see passing trains slow down or stop to allow passengers to shoot buffalo through their windows. For Native Americans, life would never be the same.

The railroad itself was a very contentious endeavor. To prevent any conflict with the western tribes, the United States government passed the Indian Trade and Intercourse Act of 1834, designating the Great Plains as land set aside for Native American nations. This, however, was canceled out in the 1850s when the U.S. reneged on the treaty when it needed the land for its expanding railroad. The re-negotiated treaties, which divided and distributed the land to specific tribes, were not much better, as they further added to the already rooted confusion. Tribes continued to hunt past their allocated lands in search of the quickly diminishing game and inevitably continued to clash with other nations as well as the ever-growing influx of settlers following the path of the railroad. As the white incursions onto their lands expanded in the 1850s, the tribes resisted as much as they could by striking back along the frontier: the Apaches in the Southwest, the Cheyenne and Arapaho in Colorado, and the Sioux—together with their western-most Teton people who called themselves the Lakota—in the Wyoming and Dakota territories.[5]

Playing up the popular distaste for war that followed the long Civil War conflict, the Native Americans doubled down their efforts of resistance in hopes of exacting a high enough price on the United States, which would hopefully be convinced to let them be. Instead, the government shifted gears into creating a whole new reservation policy in 1867 and appointed the Office of Indian Affairs to negotiate new individual treaties that would move the remaining tribes onto two extensive reservations, with some scattered smaller ones going to the less populated tribes. While many saw any resistance as futile and moved willingly, the resistance of others was only strengthened. "You might as well expect the rivers to run backward as that any man who was born a free man should be contented when penned up and denied liberty to go where he pleases," said Chief Joseph of the Nez Perce, who led his people in 1877 on a 1,500-mile march from eastern Oregon to nearly Canada trying to escape confinement on a small reservation.[6] The Indian Wars, which broke out as the Native Americans fought bitterly against reservations, would come to define American history of the West for the remainder of the nineteenth century.

After the more notable clashes such as the 1864 massacre at Sand Creek in Colorado, the 1874 Red River War in Texas, and the Apaches' struggle in New Mexico—at least until the capture of Geronimo in the 1880s—the "Indian Wars" seemed to reach their climax in June 1876 with the complete destruction of Colonel George A. Custer at the hands of Sioux and Cheyenne warriors led by Crazy Horse, Gall, and Sitting Bull. More commonly known as Custer's Last Stand, the battle, which is believed to have lasted a mere 20 minutes but which left the entire regiment of the Seventh Cavalry dead, originated 10 years prior with the Sioux resistance to the Bozeman Trail. A direct route to the supposed gold reserves of California, the trail made its way through the designated Native American lands in today's Montana, which directly interfered with tribal sovereignty. The battle between the Sioux and the U.S. Army would last for decades, solidifying expanded American military presence on the Great Plains. When more gold was discovered on the Indian reservation of South Dakota's Black Hills, Custer was ordered to oversee the forcible removal of the Sioux and Cheyenne from the lands once granted to them. Instead, the Indians decided to stay and fight, making their stand in the Bighorn River region of southern Montana. While the history of Custer's ill-advised direct assault on 4,000 Indians with his small detachment of 250 men is well known to history, the army's savage response is often overlooked.

From 1876 onwards, the tribes were hunted, starved, and attacked using, for the first time, offensive tactics as opposed to the reactive warfare that was utilized up to this point. The remaining Sioux were sought out and wiped out or forced onto reservations. Afterward, the only notable Indian battles of the Great Plains were smaller engagements against the Nez Perce in the north and the Apache in the south. But even then, these were seen as the army tidying up the last of the remaining resistance. The Indian Wars were all but over when the U.S. government passed the Dawes Act in 1887. In hopes of total assimilation, Congress attempted to break up the reservations into individual parcels of land that would be granted to each Native American family as plots of farmland. After each member of the tribe was given acreage, the remainder of the reservation lands would be sold to white settlers.

7. Black Coyote's Rifle, December 29, 1890

The profits made from the sale of these lands were to be used to help support the Native Americans' new farming endeavors. In reality, by the early 1930s, when the U.S. had taken more than two thirds of their land, the Native Americans did not receive a penny from the exchange. By accepting assimilation and leaving their tribal lands under the new act, Indians were also granted American citizenship.

While, by 1900, as many as 53,000 Native Americans were granted citizenship through accepting the Dawes Act, not all were as keen on moving from their lands. In fact, there were still many tribes throughout the plains that clung to their traditions and hoped for a better tomorrow. The Sioux, one of the first big tribes to feel the pressure of the Dawes Act, opposed it. Falsely claiming that they had gained tribal approval for the sale of surplus lands, the government opened the Sioux lands to white settlement in 1887. As thousands of settlers poured onto their lands, the tribesmen were simultaneously wary of a future grounded in farming, a process they knew little of, and the long winters without food as the plains were all but sapped of the buffalo they had depended on thus far.

As a couple of winters had passed, the Lakota people, one of the original Sioux tribes, began to fight their desperation through turning to a newly emerging Paiute prophet. Named Wovoka, the holy man promised to restore the old Sioux way of life through a ritual known as the Ghost Dance. According to the prophecy, praying to their ancestors—the ghosts—would bring them back to life and make the white invaders disappear. When the Ghost Dance movement spread through the entire Sioux reservation rapidly, the U.S. military saw it as inciting violence against the white population and ordered the arrest of the men they saw as responsible for sanctioning it. The attempted arrest and eventual killing at the hands of the U.S. Army of the Hunkpapa Lakota leader Sitting Bull would set into motion events that would forever bring about the end of all armed Native American resistance on the Great Plains. It was December 1890.

* * * * * *

When the news of Sitting Bull's death reached him, his half-brother, Chief Spotted Elk, a man considered a great peacemaker and diplomat among his Miniconjou people, suspected that he would be next. It is also evident that the chief, known as "Big Foot," did not want to share his sibling's fate. It was December 20, 1890, when the followers of the deceased Sitting Bull entered his camp with the bad news. They informed him that the time for pleading with the whites was over. Spotted Elk knew that the army was soon to follow after the refugees. The situation was dire. Black Elk of the Lakota later lamented, "My people looked pitiful ... it looked as if we might starve to death ... and there was nothing [else] we could do."[7] Chief Big Foot concurred. The next day, he and 400 of his tribe set out towards the Pine Ridge Reservation, where he hoped to unite with Chief Red Cloud and seek peace. He would never make it to his destination.

Snow was falling hard on the starving and freezing 100 warriors and nearly 300 women, children, and elderly as they made their way on the self-imposed exodus. It had been two days since Spotted Elk first complained about his health and the new rattling sound coming from deep within his chest. By now, he was being pulled along in a pony drag, unable to walk under his own strength. Five days had passed since tribal police went to arrest Sitting Bull. When the chief was being escorted out of his dwelling, one of his tribesmen took out a weapon and, in the commotion that ensued, the policeman's shot meant for the assailant had struck Sitting Bull in the head instead. Now it was up to Spotted Elk to lead the journey to find a place that provided a sanctuary for himself and his people. He just needed to get to Red Cloud.

Unbeknownst to the ailing chief, 50 Indian scouts from the Seventh Cavalry camp on the Wounded Knee Creek were exploring the countryside in hopes of finding him and his band. It was on their final search that Little Bat, Yankton Charley, and three others finally located the slow-moving group eight miles away from the military camp. After the news was delivered to Major Whiteside, "not a moment was wasted ... the bugle sounded the call of 'boots and saddles' and in exactly eleven minutes, with a light pack train following, companies A, B, I, and K ... left the camp on a gallop."[8] When his people covered half the distance, Whiteside, "wishing to avoid bloodshed if possible, sent forward Little Bat and two others, requesting the Indians to surrender at once and not to fire a gun or take the consequences."[9] Within hours, a very ailing Spotted Elk was carried over on a litter towards a mounted Whiteside. After some attempted parleying, the band had surrendered.

The Native Americans were promptly herded together, and the

march to the camp on Wounded Knee began. With two troops in advance, ambulance, Indians, and property, and two troops in the rear, the entire trek lasted no more than four hours. It was Sunday, December 28, 1890. The major would have preferred to disarm the Native Americans as soon as possible but instead opted to wait, sending for a second battalion from Pine Ridge that arrived that evening. With Colonel Forsyth's troops now in camp, the two battalions numbered 500 troops. It was time to disarm the perceived threat, yet the darkness over the camp altered that intent.[10] Instead, 300 soldiers' rations were distributed among the captives upon their arrival before they settled into their hastily erected teepees—there would be plenty of time for disarming them the following day.

According to the testimony of Dewey Beard—a Lakota tribesman present the morning of disarmament—most of the Indians willingly gave up their weapons. And as few were still standing with their rifles and knives, they did so only because they were not yet asked for them. All seemed to go smoothly until the deaf Native American, Black Coyote, did not want to give up his rifle. "The struggle for the gun was short," recalled Dewey. "The muzzle pointed upward toward the east, and the gun discharged. In an instant, a volley followed as one shot, and the people began falling."[11] The fighting that ensued went on for half an hour as both Native Americans and the troops sprung on one another with knives through the seemingly never-ending barrage of bullets. "There was a woman with an infant in her arms who was killed ... the child not knowing that its mother was dead was still nursing," proclaimed another witness, American Horse. "The women as they were fleeing with their babies were killed together, shot right through ... and after most of them had been killed a cry was made that all those who were not killed or wounded should come forth and they would be safe." The man painfully recalled, "Little boys ... came out of their places or refuge, and as soon as they came in sight, a number of soldiers surrounded them and butchered them."[12]

While the initial carnage was over fairly quickly, gunshots could be heard for at least an hour or two as "whenever a soldier saw a sign of life [he fired]." Thomas H. Tibbes, a reporter for the *Omaha World Herald* present at the scene, later reported that "Indian women and children fled into the ravine to the south, and some of them on up out of it across the prairie, but the soldiers followed them and shot them

The image, taken in 1890, shows a Native American encampment at Wounded Knee, South Dakota, with United States troops gathering up in the background. The massacre that ensued would forever end Native American resistance to white settlement in the West (photograph by Miller Studio, Library of Congress).

down mercilessly." Tibbes's recollection painted a picture much different from what U.S. newspapers wanted their readers to see. Instead of violence-prone Indians sneakily attacking unaware soldiers, this was nothing short of a massacre of primarily women and children. An eyewitness would later recall: "Nothing I have seen in my whole life ever affected or depressed or haunted me like the scenes I saw."[13]

General Forsyth was suspended from command, pending the decision of the court of inquiry regarding the events that transpired. He was, however, promptly reinstated by the secretary of war and once again placed in charge of the Seventh Cavalry. The newspapers hailed the heroes of Wounded Knee and Indian Wars as a whole. "Members of the Seventh Cavalry Again Show Themselves to Be Heroes," proclaimed one headline. Others called those in command "Masters of the Situation."[14]

7. Black Coyote's Rifle, December 29, 1890

Meanwhile, a party was sent up to Wounded Knee to bury the dead. It was later stated that "a storm had set in, followed by a blizzard, [thus] the bodies of the slain Indians lay untouched for three days, frozen stiff from where they had fallen." Some of the bodies of women and children were found slain as far as two miles away from the camp. As it was too difficult to bury them individually, a large trench was dug up on the battlefield itself, and the men and women were buried in a mass grave. Big Foot and more than half of his band were dead or seriously wounded. There were 153 confirmed deaths during the battle and nearly as many mortally wounded individuals who had saved themselves enough to die in the upcoming days. Historian Dee Brown later placed the final total of dead at very nearly 300 of the original 350 men, women, and children, with the soldiers losing 25 dead and having 39 wounded—ironically, most of them struck by their own bullets.[15]

While the next day there was an armed confrontation between the U.S. Army and the Lakota warriors from the Pine Ridge Indian Reservation to which Spotted Elk was leading his people, the events of December 29, 1890, all but ended centuries of conflicts between Native American and white American forces. Speaking about that day years later, Black Elk of the Lakota stated: "I did not know then how much was ended. When I look back now from this high hill of my old age, I can still see the butchered women and children lying heaped and scattered along the crooked gulch as plain as when I saw them with eyes still young." He added: "And I can see that something else died there in the bloody mud and was buried in the blizzard ... a people's dream died there. It was a beautiful dream."[16]

* * * * * *

Wounded Knee was undisputedly the final major episode of the long conflict of suppression of the Great Plains Indians. The years that followed directly after the massacre also marked the lowest point in the fortunes of Native Americans as a whole. The division of tribal lands quickly resumed unabated. Historian James Henretta in his survey of American history would point out how the flood of whites into South Dakota and Oklahoma left the Indians as small minorities in lands once wholly theirs—20,000 Sioux in a South Dakotan population of 400,000 in 1900, 70,000 of various tribes in a population of a million when Oklahoma became a state in 1907.[17] In fact, by the turn of the twentieth century, there were only 250,000 Native Americans in the entire nation. A children's book about Indians published around this time would put it bluntly: "The Indian pictured in these pages no longer exists."[18] It was not until around World War I, nearly 20 years later, that Indian births again surpassed deaths.

The final transition into white culture forced upon the Native Americans, which went unabated and unchallenged after the events at Wounded Knee, was mired in poverty, staggering infant mortality, and the biggest hindrance of them all, alcohol. When Congress finally abandoned the Dawes Act in the middle of the Great Depression, most Native Americans had already lost all of their land, material possessions, and honor—or, for that matter, any prospects for a better life. By that time, the situation on reservations was unpardonable, and after forcing the Native Americans to conform since the time of Wounded Knee, Congress reversed their stance and moved to allow Native American autonomy and tribal ownership. Yet even this proved to be a major debacle, as many had already assimilated into white culture, albeit unsuccessfully. And thus, by 1954, the U.S. government discovered a new approach. The "termination policy" all but eliminated any government support of the Native Americans. It backtracked on endorsing the reservation system and distributed the remaining land not already belonging to a reservation among individuals. This only added to the long history of butchered interference with Native American culture.

By 1970, Native Americans found themselves at their lowest low, perhaps since the Wounded Knee tragedy. Still mostly on reservations, the Indian population grew at four times the national rate, reaching 792,000 by the start of the decade—all while its life expectancy hovered at 46 years compared with the national average of 69.[19] The shocking statistics did not stop there: Native Americans had not only a suicide rate double the U.S. average, but also the nation's highest infant mortality rate. More than 50 percent of those living on reservations and 20 percent living in cities throughout the country did so below the national poverty level.[20] Fed up with the state of affairs, many young Native Americans joined a newly formed militant group, the American Indian Movement (AIM), based on African American organizations of the 1960s. And then came Wounded Knee, part two.

Following the massacre of 1890, the town of Wounded Knee, part of the Oglala Sioux Reservation in South Dakota, was the microcosm of the dire situation on the three-million-acre reservation. A third of all the land belonged to white settlers, another third was leased out to white cattlemen, and the remaining third belonged to the Sioux. The place of historical significance that signaled the end of Native American resistance in the West was not much better than it had been nearly a century before. In 1973, a reporter described it as "a motley collection of shacks and houses of varying degrees of decrepitude, with fine, tan, gritty dust ... coating everything and getting into mouths and lungs, contributing to the hacking cough that people seem to develop rapidly here."[21] Half of the reservation was on welfare and worked in one moccasin factory. They also lived in rural shacks, with alcohol addiction running rampant among the male population. Even the schools' dropout rate was above eight percent.

When a faction of the Sioux balked at their tribal leaders whom they saw as corrupt and favoring white interests, they reached out to AIM to bring national awareness to their plight. In February of 1973, a couple hundred American Indian Movement members occupied Wounded Knee—once more thrusting it into the national spotlight. AIM's demands of having the U.S. government honor hundreds of past treaties were met with police and military encirclement of the area, a siege that would last 71 days. Eventually, the two sides agreed to lift the blockade, and Congress decided to re-evaluate the Native American plight. Unfortunately, little changed at Wounded Knee itself. Walter LaFeber summed up Wounded Knee II as a turning point in Native American-white relations, as much as its 1890 predecessor: "Elsewhere, younger Indian leaders, inspired by the confrontation, became more active ... successfully exerting pressure to obtain a new self-governing act that empowered Native Americans themselves." He added: "They instituted lawsuits to obtain economic rights, not least the rights in some states to build enormously profitable gambling casinos."[22]

In 1972, Congress and federal courts would go on to pass additional reforms aimed at Native Americans. First came the 1972 Indian Education Act, followed by the 1975 Indian Self-Determination and Education Assistance Act. The laws granted tribes greater autonomy, especially pertaining to their children's education. For the remainder of the decade and the next, Native Americans, with copies of old and broken land treaties with the U.S., went to federal courts in a series of cases to regain recognition of their tribal lands and receive monetary compensation for past wrongs. In the 1970s, the decade of Native American resurgence, Dee Brown published a narrative history of the West as told by the Native Americans themselves. It was a first-of-its-kind written work and struck a chord with a nation jaded by the recent events of the civil rights movement, Vietnam, and the early stages of the Watergate scandal. The historian chose an event that he felt encompassed the entire history of the Native American struggle—its epitome of sorts, a high point of its debauchery—as the title of his award-winning book. *Bury My Heart at Wounded Knee* is, to this day, one of the top three best-selling books about the history of the West.

FOR FURTHER READING

When it comes to the history of the Battle of Wounded Knee or the Wounded Knee Massacre, the search for more knowledge begins and ends with Dee Brown's monumental and all-encompassing history of the Native American experience, *Bury My Heart at Wounded Knee* (1970). Ironically, the book is not strictly about the Wounded Knee Massacre—the event does not show up until the end of the book—but it is more about the events leading up to it. For a more detailed explanation or description of the event itself, one could reach for Heather Cox Richardson's *Wounded Knee: Party Politics and the Road to an American Massacre* (2010). In contrast to Brown's book, *Wounded Knee* picks up in 1850 and concentrates on the Plains Indians' road towards complete assimilation—or forced integration—of the late nineteenth century. Last by not least, the primary-source account of Private Hartford G. Clark, a guard at the Pine Ridge Agency, South Dakota, titled *Soldiering in the Shadow of Wounded Knee: The 1891 Diary of Private Hartford G. Clark* (2016), presents a great inside view of the event from those who saw it firsthand.

8

Wilson's Wilson Problem, February 22, 1913

It was nearly midnight in Mexico City. A slowly traveling automobile and its escort pierced the dense fog on the two-mile road connecting the National Palace and the Lecumberri Prison—100 armed troops on foot in front and behind it. In the back seat of the car sat two men who had called themselves the president and vice president of their nation a week prior but were now just two common prisoners. As the secret convoy was a couple of hundred yards away from its ultimate destination, shots rang out from the nearby buildings. The soldiers closed in and yelled for the two prisoners to get out of the car—they would make it inside the prison gates on foot.

Thirty-odd troops surrounded the two men and began making their way towards the fortification. The remainder of the soldiers battled more than 50 attackers, some on horseback. Between the darkness, the fog, and the commotion of gunfire, the herd around the two prisoners was overrun. The shooting lasted 20 minutes, and then, just as suddenly as it had started, it stopped. The attackers ran away into the surrounding darkness, leaving the still unnerved soldiers behind. On the ground were two dead bodies. The body of the former vice president, Pino Suárez, had many entry and exit wounds. More important was the body of the former president of Mexico, Francisco Madero, showing only one wound. A bullet had entered the back of his head and emerged through his forehead.

The General Huerta coup, which began a week prior with Madero's most trusted general overthrowing the president, was finally complete. Across town, the new leader was sharing a toast with a man who gave the night's action his blessing, the American ambassador to Mexico, Henry Lane Wilson. The relations between Mexico and the United States were about to go from bad to worse.

* * * * * *

While relegated to the dustbin of American history, the role that the United States ambassador Henry Lane Wilson played in plunging Mexico deeper into a state of a bloody revolution in 1913 is not forgotten in Mexico. The bullet that found Francisco Madero, discharged from an unspecified gun held by a faceless individual and ordered by General Huerta with the blessing of an American ambassador, was crucial to setting the ill tone between the two nations for years to come. It put into motion events that both mirrored the tense relations between the U.S. and Mexico up to that point and, more importantly, caused events that would push the nations into a new military conflict on the eve of World War I, when the U.S. could ill afford it.

The history of the United States in Latin America after the Spanish–American War (1898) is tangled with failed interventions and tribulations that even the most ardent supporters of American democracy would have a hard time justifying. In the simplest terms, from the mid-nineteenth to the early twentieth century, Latin America served as a staging ground for the U.S. evolution into a world power. The region provided a platform where foreign policy officials and intellectuals could practice the application of what political scientists at the time referred to as soft power—or "the spread of America's authority through nonmilitary means, through commerce, cultural exchange, and multilateral cooperation."[1]

For Mexico, the hand of American expansionism—or imperialism as some call it—was felt much earlier when it suffered a crippling defeat in the war against its northern neighbor in the 1840s. The Mexican–American War cost Mexico valuable land, rich in gold, silver, and other mineral deposits that would now enrich the United States instead of Mexico. Not to mention that California with its rich coast allowed the U.S. to expand its trade with Asia and continue its economic growth. For its part, Mexico fell into the struggle of one failed leadership after another while its people suffered.

It was apparent that, as America's "backyard," the Caribbean nations' stability was crucial to the security of the United States. By the late nineteenth century, many Latin American countries, Mexico included, borrowed large sums of money from European nations—especially Britain and France—to aid in their own development. The threat of defaulting on these loans and the possibility of European intervention in the region spurred the United States to adopt its own series of foreign policy doctrines.

Yet while the investments of England—the largest European investor in the region—in Central America peaked in 1913 at about $115 million, it was the U.S. investments that climbed rapidly from $21 million in 1897 to $41 million in 1908 and then to $93 million by the eve of World War I.[2] This rapid investment growth in the region was unprecedented, with almost 90 percent of the investments going to mining and cash crop plantations. All of this excluded Mexico, which by 1913 was home to 50,000 Americans, whose investments totaled about $1 billion—more than that of all other nations combined.[3] Therefore, one would be misguided to assume that the United States' involvement in Latin America was strictly driven by the desire to stabilize the region and protect it from foreign intervention.

The latter part of the nineteenth century saw Mexican and American relations evolve from open hostilities to cordial relations. During his more than 30 years (1877–1911) as the undisputed leader of the nation, Porfirio Díaz welcomed American businesses into Mexico in hopes of advancing its economic development. By the time of President William Howard Taft's term (1909–1913), American enterprise boomed under "Porfirianism," the so-called "good old days in Mexico."[4] As Mexican courts accommodated U.S. investors in developing mines, railroads, and drilling for oil, the nation's newfound prosperity benefited only a small percentage of the population while the majority of its people suffered in near peonage on large plantations belonging to the wealthy elites.

President Taft's "Dollar Diplomacy" towards Latin America was working in the United States' favor. Designed to help benefit both the people of foreign lands and American investors, the policy was aimed at deescalating the use of military presence in Latin America and instead stabilizing the area through the use of loans and economic investments. To ensure border security and protection of the United States' interests, Taft appointed a one-time ambassador to Chile, Henry Lane Wilson, to represent the U.S. government in Mexico and work closely with the friendly Díaz regime.

Yet a revolution was inevitable, for as rich as the nation of Mexico had become, the majority of the Mexican people were landless and poor. The opposition to Díaz's regime gained steam during and after the election of 1910, where the ultimate winner did not necessarily represent the people's choice. When on the eve of the election liberal reformer and visionary Francisco Madero looked likely to win, Díaz threw the young man in jail. The young Mexican argued that land had to be redistributed among the Mexican people and the nation's resources devoted to Mexican and not foreign interests. Faced with the threat of an open rebellion across the nation, Díaz resigned his post in May of 1911, shortly after once more claiming a presiden-

Henry Lane Wilson was dismissed as the ambassador to Mexico by President Woodrow Wilson, who viewed his meddling in the Mexican coup that resulted in the death of its president, Francisco Madero, as responsible for the rise of Victoriano Huerta, whom he saw as a "butcher" (National Photo Company Collection, Library of Congress)

tial electoral victory, opening the door to the Madero presidency—a man Lane Wilson called an "insane [and] dreamy idealist."[5] Wanting to remain uninvolved in Mexico's political strife, President Taft, who was amidst his reelection bid, disagreed with his ambassador and chose to recognize the new regime, no matter the dangers it posed for U.S. interests in the area.

Madero's administration quickly realized that its government lacked the funds to enforce its new policies. Things began to haltingly unravel when, in 1912, the Mexican army mutinied after not being paid their military salaries. As disorder and violence spread across the nation, President Taft's hands-off policy prevented any United States involvement, even though persistent violence threatened American lives and property. By the end of the year, U.S. shipments of goods and munitions were regularly blocked by mutinous troops at all major ports.[6] The American president's persistent inaction elicited condemnation from many American newspapers, including those published by the famous William Randolph Hearst, who had purchased a "ranch" in northern Mexico larger than Rhode Island.[7]

H.L. Wilson saw his grasp on the situation slipping, as Taft, who had just lost reelection to the Democrat Woodrow Wilson, seemed content to let his successor grapple with Mexico's growing threat and implosion. By the start of 1913, it appeared that Madero was on the verge of being overthrown by opposing factions. U.S. business interests in Mexico could ill afford an unstable situation. Without Taft's blessing, the American ambassador decided to approach the man all signs pointed to as the heir apparent, the cunning General Victoriano Huerta already scheming his way into power. The result of his actions would lead to the murder of President Madero through a single gunshot wound to the head—plunging Mexico into a state of disarray and civil war. President Woodrow Wilson, who refused to recognize Huerta's regime, would learn of H.L. Wilson's role in the tragic events and promptly dismiss the ambassador. Unfortunately, controlling the fallout from February 1913 would prove much more difficult for Wilson and the American people in the months and years to follow.

* * * * * *

The period that witnessed the overthrow and murder of the constitutionally elected Madero lasted nearly two weeks, from February 9 to February 22, 1913. In what became known in Mexican history as the "Ten Tragic Days," old supporters of Porfirio Díaz, led by his nephew Felix Díaz, organized a cuartelazo, or barracks revolt, in the capital city, with the initial intent of toppling the Mexican president overnight.[8] When the plan failed, Díaz and his followers retreated to the city's military fortress, the ciudadela or citadel, where they attacked military and civilian targets alike for the next 10 days. As all attention was drawn to the fortress, Madero's general, Victoriano Huerta, was secretly lining himself up to take control.

Although tasked with fighting Felix Díaz, Huerta secretly met with the rebel and even sent him supplies. The idea was to have the violence in the streets turn the people equally against Madero and Felix to make Huerta the real hero when he staged his coup. When the fighting started on February 9, Wilson, witnessing a revolt against the Mexican president whom he openly disliked, and sensing, based on past experience, that his superiors, with Taft at the end of his presidency, would do no more to stop him than they had previously, gave way to his penchant for meddling and used his position as a weapon against the Mexican government.[9] Wilson met with Madero's foreign minister, Pedro Lascuráin, and the apparent rebellion leader, Felix Díaz. While the meeting with the former did not yield any promises, the latter made quite an impression on the 56-year-old American ambassador. When he reported on the meetings to his superiors in Washington, he made it a point to embellish the popularity and support that Díaz was receiving in the city. In fact, his reports could not have been further from the truth, as American and international newspapers continued to report on Madero's popularity.

Having dispatched a cable to Taft requesting U.S. naval vessels be sent towards Mexico's ports for intimidation, Wilson marched into Lascuráin's office on February 10. He demanded that the Mexican government agree with the rebels under threat of intervention. In reality, the U.S. secretary of war, Henry Knox, did not see the point of dispatching a whole fleet to Mexico on Lane Wilson's whim. Only a select few ships were dispatched, and, considering the landlocked position of Mexico City, none were of any threat to the events happening in the capital.

When bullets hit the embassy building on February 12, Wilson stormed into Madero's office. He informed the president directly that nearly 3,000 American marines were loaded on naval ships headed towards Mexico. And under his authority as the representative of the American government, he could have them immediately intervene in the Mexican hostilities.

Dismissing Wilson with arguments that it was not him that was causing the carnage but the rebels, Madero went over the ambassador's head and fired off a message directly to Taft: "I have been informed that [you] ... ordered that warships shall set out for Mexico coasts with troops to be disembarked to come to this capital to give protection to

Americans." Madero assured Taft that he had things under control and that if Wilson's threat were real, "the United States would do a terrible wrong to a nation which has always been a loyal friend."[10]

Wilson was shocked when he was informed of the message and quickly sent his own dismissing Madero's telegram as "misleading." President Taft, riding out the last month of his presidency, was not willing to cause an international incident. "Perhaps Your Excellency was somewhat misinformed," he stated in his response, adding that the U.S. had no intention of sending any troops into Mexico.[11]

The U.S. ambassador now saw his favor with the American president slipping. Things were about to come to a head in Mexico, and time was of the essence. If the rumors were true, it was Madero's trusted general whom Wilson now needed to meet with. Up to this point, the cunning Huerta pretended to consult the president daily and promised a great victory against Díaz at the citadel. The general blamed the cause of his army's slowness and inaction on having to wait for proper reinforcements. He also pointed out that, after all, these were both Mexican armies fighting one another, brother versus brother, which made both sides reluctant to press the initiative. As he convinced Madero that it was perhaps better to keep Díaz encircled in the citadel for the time being, he was playing for time.

On February 16, the same day that Madero received Taft's reply, the evidence of the general's deception was finally too much even for the Mexican president to ignore. When confronted with proof that he allowed nearly 20 supply carts to enter the Díaz stronghold, Huerta defended himself by stating that had he not re-supplied his enemy, they would surely have plundered the city for food instead. He was trying to save lives. In a bewildering turn of events, Madero once more believed Huerta after the latter was seen leaving the Díaz compound the next day; this the general dismissed as an "affair of skirts." When left speechless after the last excuse, the president was comforted by Huerta, who put his arms around Madero and assured him, "You are secure in the arms of General Huerta."[12]

Having secretly met with Huerta the next day at 4:00 p.m., a satisfied Wilson promptly sent out a telegram to Washington: Madero would be removed from office within 24 hours. Instead of alerting the Mexican president of the deception, Wilson instead retired to bed early.

At 1:30 p.m. on Tuesday, February 18, 1913, President Madero and his vice president, José María Pino Suárez, were arrested during a morning cabinet meeting. They would spend the next four days in dark rooms under lock and key. Not wasting any time, Lane Wilson invited Huerta and Felix Díaz to the American embassy. In what became known as the "Pact of the Embassy," the American ambassador himself suggested a Huerta-Díaz co-regency. It was agreed that before formal elections were held—with Díaz running unopposed by Huerta—it would be the general who would become the provisional president. On February 19, Huerta forced Madero's resignation by promising the fallen leader a peaceful exile. He then maneuvered constitutional technicalities to secure from the Mexican congress the post of provisional president.

Realizing that it would be impossible to execute Madero and Suárez formally, Huerta turned to Lane Wilson for assistance and guidance. When the ambassador met with Huerta, he showed very little concern for Madero's fate, going as far as stating, "do that which [is] best for your country."[13] And with a quiet and unspoken nod of the heads, all were in agreement.

On his way home from the meeting, Wilson was greeted by Madero's wife, Sara, who pleaded for her husband's life. Unsympathetic, Wilson responded: "That is a responsibility that I do not care to undertake."[14] When Sara returned to see the ambassador the next day, on February 21, she asked him if he could relay a personal letter written to President Taft asking that he use his influence to save Madero's life. And while Wilson did indeed dispatch the letter, his intentions in the matter were not entirely pure. The U.S. ambassador noticed that the letter was not explicitly addressed to Taft. Although the letter's contents made the person it was intended for obvious, Wilson did not bother correcting the small mistake. He sent the letter along with countless other communiqués; thus it became just another item of routine diplomatic mail never to reach Taft's desk.[15]

On the evening of February 22, Ambassador Henry Lane Wilson and Victoriano Huerta presided over a reception observing the anniversary of George Washington's birthday. Wilson had already sent numerous telegrams to Taft and Secretary Knox to recognize the Huerta government. The response was not what he expected. Knox was blunt with his warning for Wilson: "General Huerta's consulting you as to the treatment of Madero gives you a certain responsibility in the matter and

... [any cruel treatment of Madero] would injure the reputation of Mexican civilization [and thus] he should be treated in a manner consistent with peace and humanity."[16]

Across town, Francisco Madero and Pino Suárez emerged from their temporary jail in the National Palace. Waiting for them were nearly 100 armed guards who would escort them to the Lecumberri Prison, barely two miles away. The men were ordered into the back of the waiting car, and the slow procession towards their destination began. The commotion started when the two men could see the gates of the prison ahead of them. In what would later be called a failed rescue attempt by the corrupt media controlled by Huerta, a guard ordered the men out of the vehicle as to make the trek into Lecumberri Prison on foot. They would never make it. While not much care was taken in the supposedly mistaken shooting of Suárez, Francisco Madero's wound pointed to a precise assassination bullet to the back of the head at close range. The would-be saviors, turned murderers, mysteriously disappeared without anybody taking the blame for what the newspapers would call an accidental killing. The Mexican people and the rest of the world were not fooled by the official statement and story of what happened. The fact that not a single other person got shot or died in the supposedly 20-minute shooting spree did not help Huerta's case.

* * * * * *

When the world found out the next morning, February 23, 1913, that Madero had been assassinated, Henry Lane Wilson's tenure in Mexico, and the status it bequeathed, was finished. Newspaper reports from those living in Mexico contradicted Wilson's telegrams of love for Huerta and hatred for Madero. Within months, accusations of his misconduct began appearing in the international press, until, after an investigation, the newly elected Democratic administration had him recalled back to the States. Faced with overwhelming public denunciations and without President Woodrow Wilson's support, Lane Wilson resigned his post. He would spend the remainder of his life arguing with anyone who would listen that he had "not interfered unnecessarily in Mexico's internal affairs" and had done "everything possible to save Madero's life."[17]

Yet, the bullet fired into Madero's brain on February 22 had much more significant consequences for the United States than the dismissal of the one man who could be held responsible for perpetrating it. In terms of immediate causes, the situation enabled by Ambassador Wilson pitted a morally driven and idealistic American president against Huerta, a man who epitomized political corruption, opportunity, and malice. Woodrow Wilson entered the White House in 1913 with promises of a foreign policy based on moral principles and "making [American] influence felt among the nations of the world, not by fear of our battleships, but by the powerful plea of a good example."[18] In another statement issued shortly after taking office, Wilson made it very clear that he would not support strongmen leaders who assumed power through force. With regards to Latin America, his administration would "cultivate the friendship and deserve their confidence," yet only towards those nations with just governments that rested "upon the consent of the governed."[19] While Francisco Madero was democratically elected and hence the definition of Wilson's perfect ally in Latin America, recognizing Huerta would go against everything he believed in. The former Mexican president's murder had left Wilson in a peculiar situation that would lead the nation towards unfortunate circumstances between the two countries, not just for the remainder of his presidency but for decades to come.

Historian John Milton Cooper, Jr., would later write that "the most pressing diplomatic concern for the United States in 1914 was not the European war but Mexico, with its political and social turmoil."[20] While formerly the United States had recognized revolutionary governments in the Western Hemisphere if they were able to keep the peace and protect foreign rights, Wilson now drew the line with Huerta, whose cunning and ruthless coup he detested.

Speaking to the nation, President Wilson made it known that he would not "extend the hand of welcome to anyone who obtains power in a sinister republic by treachery and violence."[21] Publicly referring to Mexico as "Huerta's government of butchers," Wilson demanded that Huerta cease all hostilities and open the nation to new elections, removing himself from the running. When the Mexican leader refused, the American president, still ashamed of former ambassador Wilson's role in the killing of President Madero, refused to acknowledge Huerta, whose government he saw as illegitimate. Adopting a policy of "watchful waiting," Woodrow Wilson continued going against his European allies in recognizing Huerta's government—something that most

European nations had already done. Instead, he proceeded to block military supplies going to the Mexican leader from those same European allies on the ground of invoking the Monroe Doctrine. Instead he began secretly arming Huerta's domestic enemies and three separate military factions led by Venustiano Carranza, Francisco "Pancho" Villa, and Emiliano Zapata. Wilson was unwilling to pick between the Mexican strongmen vying to take power from Huerta. His only aim was to hinder the current Mexican leader's power to force a leadership change that would hopefully be based on democratic ideals. His "watchful waiting" would come to an abrupt end in April 1914.

When the American gunboat *Dolphin* landed at Tampico, Mexico, to purchase fuel supplies, the crew was arrested by Huerta's soldiers and marched off to jail to the jeers of the crowds. And while the Huerta hastily released the American sailors and apologized for the misunderstanding, he refused to bend to the American admiral's demand that the American flag be recognized with a proper 21-gun salute. Before the matter was allowed to escalate, the U.S. learned of a German ship loaded with munitions headed straight for the Mexican port of Veracruz. Without waiting for congressional consent, Wilson sent American soldiers to occupy the port city. For the first time since American general Winfield Scott landed at Veracruz in 1847 during the Mexican–American War, U.S. troops occupied the city once more. Although unclear who fired the first shots in 1914, the fighting between the two armies left 126 Mexican soldiers dead, with another 195 wounded, while the U.S. suffered 19 casualties.[22]

Rescued from escalating the war beyond one military incident by mediation from Argentina, Brazil, and Chile, Wilson came out of the scuffle, apart from some negative press, mostly unscathed. However, Huerta's weakness led other militaristic factions within his country to gain on him and force his abdication to Europe in late 1914. With the war in Europe heating up, Wilson took his foot off the gas. He backtracked on his self-righteousness by recognizing the new provisional president, Venustiano Carranza, whose fight against Huerta he once supported despite never regarding him as his proper replacement. But things only went from bad to worse for Wilson and the United States as a whole. The unstable political situation left in the aftermath of the bullet that killed former president Francisco Madero in February of 1913 was nowhere near stable and soon spilled over the American border.

Bullets That Changed America

No sooner did Carranza take over the government as its de facto leader than his two generals, Emiliano Zapata and Pancho Villa, rose against him and seized Mexico City. After negotiating the removal of U.S. troops from Veracruz, Carranza seized much of the U.S. military equipment willingly left behind. He would use these materials and the newly found respect of the Mexican people to win victories against his defectors. While Zapata was quickly confined to a specific region of Mexico, Pancho Villa, furious about the U.S. meddling he saw as the cause of the instability in Mexico, decided to unleash a bloody crusade against the northern power. Woodrow Wilson's flip-flopping and fumble first weakened and ultimately brought down Huerta's government, then recognized an equally oppressive one led by Carranza—far from resembling a democracy that the U.S. leader promised Latin American countries. Hoping to draw American intervention that might backfire against Carranza, in January of 1916, Villa and his followers hauled 17 young American engineers from a train in Mexico and shot 16 of them.[23] By March, he would lead a raid across the Rio Grande into Columbus, New Mexico, killing 19 Americans.

With 1916 being an election year, the pressure was mounting on Wilson to do something about Villa's attacks on U.S. soil. It seemed that the U.S. and Mexico were once again headed for war. In 1846 a claim—disputed by some—of American blood being shed on American soil pushed the American people into a conflict with their southern neighbor. This time there were no doubts as to the location of the violent attack. President Wilson's unwavering refusal to follow his predecessors' policies in Mexico, his failure to oust the corrupt Huerta from the presidency in 1913, and his more-active-than-not "watchful waiting" was about to involve the United States in a military conflict they could hardly afford. Wilson and the American people's real and more dangerous test was eagerly awaiting them across the Atlantic.

The American president ordered General John J. Pershing and his 10,000 troops to capture Villa in Mexico. This proved more difficult than initially thought. For one, Carranza, outraged by the United States dispatching a military expedition into his nation, refused the American forces the use of the country's railroad system. As Villa led the Punitive Expedition forces deeper into Mexico on what was quickly becoming a wild goose chase, tensions between the two countries grew at an alarming rate. Nine months into what was now obviously a failed endeavor and after countless skirmishes with Carranza's Mexican troops, Wilson, not wanting to risk a full-scale war with Mexico, recalled Pershing's forces back across the northern border. It was January 1917; within three months, the American general and his troops, along with countless others, would be shipped off to fight in World War I.

Had the events of February 1913 gone a different way and had Ambassador Henry Lane Wilson not given his blessing to the assassination of former Mexican president Francisco Madero, perhaps history would have taken the two nations in a different direction. Potentially, Huerta would have sent the fallen leader into exile as was the initial plan, and the ostensibly democratic election favoring Huerta would have taken place. Wilson would no longer have had a pretext to make Mexico the test case for his "Moral Diplomacy." As was the case, due to the violent way Madero met his end, and with the American ambassador's meddling to boot, Wilson could not bring himself to support Huerta. This, in turn, led to his desire to compensate for what he saw as American failure in Mexico. Going from one blunder to another instead of promoting affection for his moral diplomacy south of the border, Wilson only exacerbated the tensions between the two nations. There is no hiding that Wilson subjected Mexico to two armed invasions during his presidency, which cost lives on both sides. In the words of Eric Foner, "Mexico was a warning that it might be more difficult than Wilson assumed to use American might to reorder the internal affairs of the other nations, or to apply moral certainty to foreign policy."[24] The tensions stemming from the Mexican–American War of the 1840s, having witnessed a cooling period in the late nineteenth century, were extended into the 20th, setting a precedent that has continued ever since.

For Further Reading

One of the most accessible histories on Mexican–American relations from the assassination of Francisco Madero until 1917 is John S.D. Eisenhower's *Intervention! The United States and the Mexican Revolution, 1913–17* (1993). A more recent study that concentrates more on the Wilson years dealing with Mexico is Jeff Guinn's 2021 *War on the Border: Villa, Pershing, the Texas Rangers, and an American Invasion.* Thoroughly researched, it is written in a popular history style that reads more like a thriller than a historical account. For contextual information, John Milton Cooper, Jr.'s, *Pivotal Decades: The United States, 1900–1920* (1990), provides an excellent narrative of the U.S. situation on the eve of and after the events discussed in this chapter. On the other side, one can not go wrong with *The Oxford History of Mexico* by William Beezley (2010).

9

An Afternoon Holdup,
April 15, 1920

Alessandro Berardelli, being in his forties, might have been too old for this kind of a job. Still, he had a good relationship with his superior, Fred. A. Parmenter, and the pay was good. Employed as a special guard in the Slater & Morrill Shoe Co. of South Braintree, Massachusetts, Alessandro walked ahead of the company paymaster as they began their usual walk towards the lower factory building. It was 3:00 in the afternoon of April 15, 1920, and a pleasant spring day by every definition. In Parmenter's right hand was a leather bag containing approximately $20,000 in cash. The guard stopped as the two men were about to cross the street directly in front of the neighboring Rice & Hutchins shoe factory on Pearl Street, South Braintree—just 20 yards from their shoe plant and final destination. Unaware that he was now crossing the street by himself, Parmenter found himself alone in the middle of the road.

Two men who were lazily leaning against an iron fence in front of the plant sprang forward and ran up to the paymaster. As Berardelli realized what was going on, he leapt towards Parmenter. One of the two men drew a gun and fired. Before he could make it to his manager's side, Alessandro was cut down by the first bullet, which found its mark just below his heart. The second shot struck the right breast of a panic-stricken and seemingly paralyzed Parmenter. One of the shooters checked the leather bag containing thousands of dollars in envelopes that were ready to be distributed to the 400 employees of the factory. The other man's gaze followed the paymaster, blood streaking down the front and back of his shirt, trying to make his way across the street and away from the bandits.[1]

In all the commotion, a car—which had been parked nearby all day—skidded onto the street. A third man lunged from behind a large

---

pile of bricks at a nearby empty lot and began shooting his rifle as he made his way towards the car. Witnesses scattered for cover. The sickly looking young man driving the vehicle beckoned the man with the leather bag to get into the car. It was then that they realized that the initial robber with the gun had gone after the paymaster. The getaway vehicle with three men pulled up to the third armed robber as he stood over the fallen Parmenter, pumping additional shots into his back. Someone screamed, "Call the police!" The dark-complexioned third man, with his gun now devoid of bullets, grabbed the handle of the car door as it pulled up. He got inside. Alessandro Berardelli, lying on the ground in a pool of blood, tried but failed to cover his face as the tires kicked up dirt in his direction. He had only a couple of minutes to live.

* * * * *

Nicola Sacco and Bartolomeo Vanzetti were by no means famous—at least until the last seven years of their lives when they became front-page news in the lead-up to execution for the murder in April 1920 of a paymaster and his guard in Braintree, Massachusetts. By the time of their deaths on August 23, 1927, their names would become synonymous with the anti-radical sentiment that had gripped the nation. In fact, their story—of being guilty only of being immigrants and anarchists, of their arrest three weeks after the Braintree shootings, of their trial and conviction, and of the seven years in jail full of appeals—is still prominently mentioned in nearly every American high school history textbook. Before the public's conscience shifted towards a collective struggle against the forces of the Great Depression, which began with the stock market crash of 1929, it was the fallout from the shots that rang out at Braintree that occupied national news.

The events that followed the arrest of the two immigrant anarchists for the murder of Berardelli and Parmenter brought to the surface America's struggle with xenophobia and nativism. There could no longer be any denial of the nation's fears and apprehensions. In a sense, the fallout from the Braintree event was the culmination of the anti-immigrant attitudes growing in the United States since the late 1800s. With the case of Sacco and Vanzetti, it all finally boiled over. America of the 1920s had a problem, and Sacco and Vanzetti's case—whether they were guilty or not, which is still disputed—was the nation's way of admitting it. Yet, it by no means meant that America was ready to face its problem head-on. In truth, when the trial against the two men began, the United States was admitting 805,000 immigrants through its borders each year. By the time of the men's execution in 1927, the new quota system put in place after the 1920 Braintree event had limited that number to 150,000.[2] And while the story of Sacco and Vanzetti is still taught in American classrooms as a time of great social upheaval that once was, perhaps it is simply a reminder of a nation's inner struggle, which comes out to the open once in a while to remind us of its existence.

The late nineteenth century witnessed an influx of new immigrants arriving on American shores. While up to this point most of the men and women—the literate and the skilled—came from northern or western European countries such as England, Ireland, or Germany, the new wave stemmed from southern or eastern Europe. These Italians, Russians, Poles, and Greeks arriving in the United States were also no longer predominantly Protestant, as were their predecessors. Instead, the now typically illiterate and unskilled individuals were Catholic, Orthodox, or Jewish. Instead of coming from democratic nations, they also brought experiences and ideals stemming from living their entire lives in countries with histories of communism, anarchism, and socialism. Perhaps most importantly, while the old immigrants were quick to assimilate, these new immigrants were very reluctant to do the same.

Many prominent and outspoken members of society claimed that the immigration of people of presumably inferior races was weakening the nation's social fabric. Historian Eric Foner pointed out in his study on the history of American "liberty" how, according to an 1890 economist Francis Amasa Walker, immigrants were "beaten men from beaten races, representing the worst failures in the struggle for existence." Meanwhile, an Ohio newspaper from the same year claimed that cities were being overrun by foreigners who "have no true appreciation of the meaning of liberty."[3] Yet, as the ever-growing numbers of "undesirables" increased, so did the need for their cheap labor in industries such as steel production, textiles, and coal mining. This, however, came to a screeching halt at the end of World War I. While the nation had fewer unskilled jobs to fill and too many unskilled workers, attitudes of limiting immigration took center stage in the nation's psyche. The fact that many critics of the war were socialists, anarchists, or members of the Industrial Workers of the World (IWW), a union made up of and mainly representing unskilled immigrant workers, did not help their cause.

Bullets That Changed America

During World War I, President Woodrow Wilson considered any dissent against American war policies dangerous to national security. As the Socialist Party under Eugene V. Debs declared that this was a war for the benefit of the wealthy class, the president was quick to label them as treacherous, linking the party and its ideology with duplicity. Subconsciously, or perhaps not so much, the American people associated the dissent with mostly socialist and working-class individuals and union activity, lumping it all with foreigners spreading radical ideas brought over from the Old World. It did not matter that "socialism," or the desire for more government oversight of industry, was different from both communism with its complete abandonment of private property and anarchism advocating the total abolition of all government in favor of a new voluntary society. In the public mind exhausted by World War I, the ideologies were all lumped together by one common thread, immigration.

Everything was set for the nation to implode. Stirred up by a successful Russian Revolution that culminated with an overthrow of the Russian monarchy, the American people were put on high alert against anything they perceived as foreign, whether communist, socialist, or anarchist. The president only fueled this paranoia through the passage of the 1917 Espionage Act. The new legislation was bluntly aimed at curtailing immigrants' fundamental freedoms in fear that their dissent could in some way be treacherous. "There are citizens of the United States, I blush to admit, born under other flags but welcomed under our neutralization laws ... who have poured the poison of disloyalty into the very arteries of our national life," stated Wilson in his December 7, 1915, State of the Union address. "Such creatures of passion, disloyalty, and anarchy must be crushed out."[4] The Sedition Act of 1918, which was an extension of the Espionage Act, directly targeted anyone who criticized the government and, more importantly, created a prerogative for the attorney general, A. Mitchell Palmer, to monitor and deport any immigrant radicals deemed dangerous.

It was inevitable that the country would be frenzied into hysteria following the end of the war in 1919, when a series of bombs targeting government and law enforcement officials exploded around the nation. In the end, a mail clerk intercepted 36 mail bombs before they could be delivered to other notable citizens.[5] Then on June 2, 1919, a bomb exploded in front of Attorney General Palmer's home in Washington,

D.C. And while the explosion ironically only took the life of the anarchist who planted it, it was enough for A. Mitchell Palmer to make every effort to suppress any threat of radicalism throughout the nation. By January 1920, Palmer, assisted by a young J. Edgar Hoover of the new Federal Bureau of Investigation, coordinated raids on offices of radical organizations in every major city in the United States. Trampling people's basic civil rights, government officials invaded people's homes and jailed suspects without proper due process of law. Just a month prior, in December 1919, the steamer *Buford* sailed for Russia with 249 deportees, none of whom saw a courtroom or a simple trial.[6]

Yet as is always the case with any abuse of power, it quickly breeds resistance. The massive violations of legal proceedings brought protests from liberal Protestant clergymen, law school faculty members, and even the Supreme Court by January 26, 1920.[7] Still, although short-lived, the Red Scare, as the press dubbed it, only fed the public suspicions of immigrants and foreigners of any kind. It was as if a wave of often unfounded fear and nativist sentiment of "Keep America for Americans" swept the nation.[8] When the payroll shooting occurred in Braintree, all it took was for one of the witnesses to state that the robbers looked Italian. Barely a month later, it proved enough to get Sacco and Vanzetti, two known anarchists and Italian immigrants, arrested for the crime. Although the two would become martyrs of the leftist world, more modern FBI ballistic reports do show that Sacco at least was highly likely guilty of the crime. Still, as historian Kenneth C. Davis pointed out years later, Nicola Sacco and Bartolomeo Vanzetti had three strikes against them in the late spring of 1920. They were Italian. They were immigrants. And they were anarchists.[9]

* * * * * *

It is almost ironic that history remembers the death of the wrong two men. While the real victims, Alessandro Berardelli and Fred A. Parmenter, are all but lost to posterity, it is their alleged murderers who grace the pages of today's school textbooks. Perhaps, this is not surprising considering that the number of homicides and armed robberies in the 1920s jumped 40 percent—partially due to the rise of organized crime stemming from the enactment of Prohibition.[10] Therefore, the death of a paymaster and his guard could easily get absorbed into the greater crime statistics of the decade. At least it would have had the national climate not been amped up on fear and hysteria. As such, the real story of the Braintree holdup does not lie in its immediate causes but is more significantly grounded in the events that followed. Events that unraveled rather quickly yet lasted for seven years until the ultimate execution of two Italian anarchists.

It was the first week of May 1920, barely three weeks since the shootings in front of the Slater & Morrill Shoe Company. Bridgewater Police Chief Michael Steward later remembered having a hunch. Examining the Braintree crime scene, the officer thought that he had seen a similar crime with a parallel execution—albeit a failed one—before. That other holdup from a few months prior had put him on to one Mike Boda. The man who would eventually become the main suspect in the 1920 Wall Street bombing, which killed nearly 40 people, was already suspected of subversive activities in the area. Yet, no matter how much he tried, Steward could not pin anything on him.

Still, the police chief had his officers keep an eye on the suspect's car, which had been left at a local garage for repairs. In his mind, the Braintree crime followed the same pattern of a crime for which Boda was his main suspect. Namely, it involved four Italian-looking men, three on foot and one in a gateway car. Still, the description of the men and the witnesses of the failed December 1919 holdup scene were lackluster at best. However, the same could not be said of the plethora of statements he was able to get from various eyewitnesses at the April 15, 1920, shooting in Braintree. This time, Chief Steward at least had a better idea of whom he was looking for. This would later be disputed, as the only real evidence he possessed was that the men were foreign-looking, perhaps Italian. He now hoped that whoever came to pick up Boda's car from the repair shop might fit some of the more detailed descriptions he had on file from the second crime.

When Boda and three other Italian men showed up to pick up the car on May 5, 1920, they suspected something was amiss. It was already late in the evening, yet still light enough for the garage owners to see them coming. As they approached the glass front door, Boda was quick to notice the proprietor's wife, Mrs. Johnson, quickly move to the corner of the room and pick up the telephone. As the owner told the four men that their car, while fixed, could not be driven that day due to an expired registration, the suspicious men chose not to wait. Splitting up,

Boda and a man named Orciana hopped on a motorcycle and left the scene.

Meanwhile, the other two Italians opted for public transportation. As they approached a nearby trolley stop, they were discouraged from waiting for the car to arrive as they could hear a faint police siren drawing nearer. Their suspicions of the garage owners were correct. The two men walked briskly to another railcar stop nearly a mile away, hurrying away from the scene. Nicola Sacco and Bartolomeo Vanzetti's ride would be cut short that day.

As the trolley made its first stop on the way to Brockton, it was boarded by police officer Michael Connolly. Upon seeing two foreign men who appeared agitated and perspiring, he decided to arrest them. When questioned by the court, the officer stated that he had done so on the basis that the men looked suspicious.[11] Once they were brought to the station, Mrs. Johnson identified the men as the two who had come with Boda and Orciana to her shop the evening of May 5. When arrested, Sacco carried a loaded .32 Colt automatic pistol, Vanzetti a loaded .38 Harrington and Richardson revolver; Sacco also possessed a notice, written in Italian, of an upcoming anarchist rally at which Vanzetti was scheduled to speak.[12] Also in Sacco's possession were several bullet cases matching the Winchester .32 casings found at the Braintree crime scene. As for Vanzetti's gun, it was the same gun carried by the slain Braintree guard, a weapon that had gone missing from the scene of the crime.

Yet, there were factors casting doubt on the role the two men might have had in the holdup. For one, the money was never found on their persons or amongst any of their belongings. And while it does not automatically point to their innocence, the two men had no criminal record prior to being arrested for the said crime. The case was further complicated when another person—a member of organized crime—later claimed to have shot the paymaster and the guard. In the end, nearly 100 witnesses either claimed to have seen the two men somewhere else on the day of the shooting or could not with complete certainty say that it was them who they saw coming to the heist. Yet, a large enough number of witnesses said the two men were the ones they saw commit the crime.

With lackluster alibis and in the face of what was deemed sufficient incriminating evidence, the defense was helpless. On July 14, 1921, after a month of court hearings, the jury took less than five hours to find Sacco and Vanzetti guilty of robbery and the murder of Alessandro Berardelli and Fred. A. Parmenter. It might seem odd—and did for many—that it would take so little time for the jurors to come up with their verdict in a trial that lasted nearly two months and included well over a hundred testimonies.

As per historians James West Davidson and Mark Hamilton Lytle, the controversy did not end with the jury's decision: "Six years of appeals turned a small-town incident of robbery and murder into a major international uproar."[13] For many, Sacco and Vanzetti were guilty only of having radical beliefs and being immigrants. The poet Edna St. Vincent Millay donated proceeds from her poem "Justice Denied in Massachusetts" to their defense and went as far as personally appealing to the state governor on their behalf. For the next six years on death row, the two men published numerous letters that further endeared them to the general public. Historians have since pointed out that the two seized men, supposed criminals, instead came to be regarded as martyrs or even philosophers.[14] While Sacco and Vanzetti stayed behind bars, unsuccessfully appealing their case, "thousands of liberals, criminal lawyers, legal scholars, civil libertarians, radicals, labor leaders, prominent socialites, and spokesmen for immigrant groups rallied for [their release]."[15]

With thousands of armed police patrolling around Boston and many more protesting in front of the governor's mansion, the two men were led towards their respective ends by the electric chair on August 23, 1927. As ropes surrounded the prison and police kept the loud protesters at bay, Sacco was strapped into the electric chair. His friend Vanzetti would follow minutes later. Fifteen thousand people were reported to have gathered in New York's Union Square to pay their silent respects to the two men. Even more silent vigils were reported in major European cities. As Davidson and Lytle pointed out in their analysis of the case, "all awaited the news of the fate of 'a good shoemaker and a poor fish peddler.'"[16]

* * * * * *

It would be difficult to distinguish between causation and correlation when it comes to the effects of the bullet fired at Alessandro Berardelli on April 15, 1920. What cannot be disputed is that the shot immortalized a time in American history where two accused criminals managed to expose the nation's flaws. Eric Foner probably said it best many years after the fact when he wrote:

> It demonstrated how long the Red Scare extended into the 1920s and how powerfully it undermined basic American freedoms. It reflected the fierce cultural battles that raged in many communities during the decade ... [with their outcome] ... symbolizing the nativist prejudices and stereotypes that haunted immigrant communities [and perhaps still do].[17]

Perhaps, Sacco and Vanzetti were not the right men to evoke such a response from the public. A public that, by the 1920s, was already showing distrust towards the government—a harbinger for what was to come decades later in the shadow of Vietnam and Watergate. In 1961, new ballistic tests showed decisively that the pistol found on Sacco on the day of his arrest was indeed the one used to kill Berardelli. So maybe Sacco and Vanzetti were guilty of the crime for which they were accused. Still, by the time of their execution, that no longer seemed to matter. They came to represent an idea more significant than just shooting two men and stealing nearly $20,000.

In response to nativist pressure, the U.S. Congress created and passed the Emergency Quota Act of 1921. Between the Braintree shooting and subsequent arrest of Sacco and Vanzetti and the year of their execution in 1927, the United States reduced the number of persons allowed admittance to the nation by nearly three-quarters of the number previously allowed. Further amended in 1924, the law limited immigration from every European country to two percent of the number of its nationals living in the United States in 1890.[18] While it might have seemed fair on the surface, the law was explicitly designed to discriminate against eastern and southern Europeans such as Sacco and Vanzetti, as this new wave of immigration did not start to arrive at the American shores in large numbers until after the chosen cut off year (which itself was later moved to 1920). The disparity can be best shown by the effect the new National Origins Act of 1924 had on specific nations. Namely, the combined quota for Russia and Italy was less than that for Norway, while the combined quota for Poland and Greece was less than that for Sweden.[19]

In the shadow of the national frenzy caused by post-war xenophobia, the Red Scare, and anti-immigrant opinions, which thanks to

Taken in 1927, the picture depicts riot squad guards in front of the Dedham courthouse on the date of Sacco and Vanzetti's hearing. Riots protesting against the two anarchists being put on trial erupted around the world prior to and after the verdict was officially announced (*New York World-Telegram* and the *Sun* Newspaper Photograph Collection, Library of Congress).

the Sacco and Vanzetti case were front-page news for nearly the entire decade, a revival of the nation's most nativist group was growing unopposed. While the "new" Klan was started in 1915 by ex-preacher William J. Simmons, it was not until the early 1920s when millions of Americans joined the hooded order.[20] Unlike the Klan of the old, which concentrated its hatred only towards African Americans, this new Klan was very much a product of its time. The organization's activities varied very much according to its geographical location and what its members perceived to be a threat to their way of life. As such, as historian Walter LaFeber points out, "the Klan was no longer primarily a white supremacist group. ... Its chief targets in the 1920s were immigrants and Catholics."[21]

All of a sudden, the Klan preached ideals that appealed to a great many people who believed that immigration had threatened the social fabric of the nation. Ideas that were no longer directed at one race or towards one geographical region. As Simmons put it, "the dangers were in the tremendous influx of foreign immigration, tutored in alien dogmas and alien creeds, slowly pushing the native-born white American population into the center of the country, there to be ultimately overwhelmed and smothered."[22] Luckily, the biased group's criminal activities led to its downfall. Through numerous arrests, most notably that of its newest leader, who was found guilty of abducting and molesting a young woman, the Klan's membership began to significantly diminish by 1928. By the end of the decade, the once quite dominant group in various states' politics was in shambles. Aiding in this outcome was the appeasement of national nativist feelings through the multiple quota laws and the final verdict and execution in the case of Sacco and Vanzetti.

The fears brought on and exacerbated by the fallout from the armed robbery at Braintree, Massachusetts, concurrent with the rise and fall of the "new" Klan, were all forgotten on October 29, 1929. In what history dubbed "Black Tuesday," investors traded some 16 million shares on the New York Stock Exchange in a single day, wiping out billions of dollars in investments.[23] The United States and the rest of the world began its downward spiral into the greatest and longest economic depression in the history of the industrial world. Alessandro Berardelli, lying in the middle of the street on April 15, 1920, struggling to breathe and choking on his own blood, could not have known any of that. The loyal guard would miss what his death would come to represent for the decade preceding the most infamous time in American history, the same way that history would miss the significance of him being shot and dying that day. Simply stated, without Berardelli and Parmenter, there is no Sacco and Vanzetti. The dying man simply looked ahead as the car with the men who shot him disappeared around the corner. He closed his eyes, never to open them again.

For Further Reading

While by no means a book dedicated entirely to the event, *After the Fact: The Art of Historical Detection* (1992) by James West Davidson and Mark Hamilton Lytle dedicated an entire chapter to the infamous case of Sacco and Vanzetti. The story and the historical analysis and evaluation are written in a very inquisitive, true-crime style so popular in the twenty-first century. It also places the event very much in context of the national history and takes the account presented in this work to whole new levels by dedicating more time and detail to the little intricacies that could not make it into this work. There is also Francis Russell's *Sacco & Vanzetti: The Case Resolved* (1986), which makes a definitive case for the men's guilt. There is also an invaluable collection of relevant documents and selected analyses of the event in Michael M. Topp's *The Sacco and Vanzetti Case: A Brief History with Documents* (2004), published by Bedford St. Martin's. Last but not least, a more objective account of the case can be found in *The Sacco-Vanzetti Affair: America on Trial* (2011) by Moshik Temkin.

10

The Unfortunate Bonus,
July 28, 1932

It was just another day in Anacostia Flats "Hooverville," a swampy, muddy, and miserable plot of land directly across from the Capitol and adjacent to the Anacostia River flowing through the nation's capital. Not that there was much to see. Looking towards the very emblem of American democracy, one first had to look through endless huts and makeshift shelters with their tin and thatched straw roofs constructed from materials dragged in from a nearby junk pile. Scattered amongst the low-lying village were a few leftover and badly demolished two- and three-story buildings that belonged to another long-ago century. Below their shadow lived nearly 10,000 veterans of World War I, together with their wives and children. They came to the capital to demand that their war bonuses be paid ahead of the previously agreed-upon 20-year maturing period. It was the Great Depression, and their families needed the money then. The scars left over from the war, both physical and emotional, proved that they had earned it. But on that day and at that hour, their past deeds and sacrifices for their nation did not matter. It was 10:00 a.m. Their eviction had begun.

General Glassford's police and treasury agents were having a hard time clearing out the skeletonized buildings. The hundreds of veterans surrounding them were beginning to swell to thousands as more and more people came out to see the commotion. The attention was turned to a nearby building where a small group of veterans staged their resistance by ignoring police cries and entered the building carrying a large U.S. flag. Someone from the crowd threw a brick at the police officers attempting to follow the protesters into the structure. Several of the officers turned towards the crowd, their guns drawn. "There's a fight!" an elderly man cried out.[1] As more bricks began flying, another veteran shouted, "Give the cops hell!"[2] Armed with clubs, bricks, or anything they could grab, the mob, made up of tired and fed-up veterans, attacked the police. As one officer dropped to the floor with his head smashed in, he was quickly trampled under the feet of the mob trying to get to his fellow policemen.

Glassford was himself thrown to the ground in the melee, his face badly cut, and his police badge ripped off his coat. A riot call of bellowing whistles that could be heard blocks away brought additional police forces to the scene. It was now hundreds of constables against thousands of veterans of World War I. "Be peaceful, men! Be calm!" yelled the general, who barely made it up from the ground under his strength. "Let's not throw any more bricks. They're mighty hard and hurt," added the officer, shocked at the situation unfolding before him. Looking down at the patrolman lying near him with his face covered in blood, Glassford spoke in what seemed like whispers, "You've probably killed one of my best officers."[3] All but a few heard him. "Lots of us were killed in France!" yelled back a nearby veteran.

On the second floor of the building directly in front of Glassford was another altercation. One which would have far-reaching implications for the history of the nation going forward. Officers Miles Zamanezck and George Shinault were trapped in a room with no way of escaping. The angry mob was closing in on them. They were now at the door blocking the policemen's exit. Without speaking, the officers looked at each other, nodded, and drew their revolvers. Angry men with clubs and broken-off concrete pieces in their hands rushed into the small room. "Let's get them!" shouted one of the men.[4] The mob filled the room as six shots rang out. One bullet ripped open William Hushka's chest. Intended or not, the bullet struck its mark directly into the man's heart. As the World War I veteran dropped to the floor, another bullet struck his once brother-in-arms, Eric Carlson. He would die hours later. By then, the Bonus March was no longer a local issue. And the nation and its history would be changed forever.

* * * * * *

The year 1932 was the worst of the Great Depression since the stock market crashed in 1929. It was the year of one of the most important organized protests in the nation's history. And it was also the year that finally sealed Herbert Hoover's fate as a one-term president. The final nail in the coffin came with the president's interference and misman-agement of the nearly 20,000 World War I veterans and their families—the aptly called Bonus Expeditionary Force, or the Bonus Army. The men and their families had made their way to Washington, D.C., in June of 1932 to petition Congress for early payouts of their war bonuses. And while local forces initially managed the protest, the killing of two men by Capitol Police officers forced Hoover's hand into federal interference. By the time it was all over, in the eyes of his people, Herbert Hoover had become their leader and president in name only. His long career as one of the greatest humanitarians in the nation's history was over. His legacy as president was tarnished forever.

The Great Depression was not Hoover's fault. In fact, he had only been president for a few months when the stock market crashed in 1929. Yet, by the last day of his presidency, his name would become synonymous with standing in the cold rain or snow waiting for a bowl of soup or a piece of bread, or getting up each morning to wait for hours at the docks trying to get work only to be turned away. And perhaps most importantly, it became intertwined with the growing perception of a failed government, one indifferent towards its people's suffering. In all fairness, while not the first president to face a massive economic depression, he was the first one who tried to intervene and overcome it—albeit late, according to many. History had taught the executive office to mostly ride out the storm when it came to recessions and depressions.

Railroad construction took over as the primary growth industry after the American Civil War, and the companies that controlled it became the largest employers of the vast network of American farmers. It seemed that no bank or industry could go wrong with investing stock in rail companies. Until the banking firm of Jay Cooke, one of the government's chief financiers of railroad construction, overextended its spending and declared bankruptcy in 1873, ushering a national economic panic as many banking firms and companies followed suit. President Ulysses S. Grant created a blueprint for other Republican leaders in times of financial crisis: he sided with business leaders. While Congress attempted to infuse the economy with more cash to make it more accessible to the common man, Grant vetoed the bill in 1874. He disagreed with any short-term benefits for the ailing people, lest it cause inflation and hurt the nation's businesses in the long term. As the bankers and industrialists cheered his decision, the nation quietly slipped into a five-year depression. Without direct government stimulus, business and production would bring the nation back up onto its feet—or so the president hoped.

Ironically, Grant's support for moving the country back towards the gold standard instead of printing an additional $100 million in the paper currency as the Congress wanted in 1874 would lead the nation to unprecedented economic growth in the 1880s once it came out of the depression. Following this belief of minimal government direct assistance, President Grover Cleveland learned the hard way that placing complete faith in hopes of the business sector pulling the nation out of a recession may not be the best course of action. When the United States once more entered an economic crisis in 1893 caused by the contraction of an exhausted business cycle, Cleveland would take the brunt of the blame for lacking empathy towards the suffering masses when he sent federal troops to quell strikes in Pennsylvania, Ohio, and Illinois. And in what proved to be a pattern, the U.S. economy righted itself once more a few years later, albeit with the Republican Party's ability to respond to crisis a bit tarnished. Still, by the time it was Hoover's turn to face a depression, it seemed that this one too would follow the same pattern.

Contrary to public opinion, President Hoover was not as much inactive when it came to pulling the nation out of this new depression as he was simply slow to overcome his strictly republican laissez-faire beliefs. His biggest initial flaw was his inability to see past his support of what he called "rugged individualism," where a person needed to be self-reliant and, above all else, free from any government charity. Government intervention would have to wait. As a sign of his belief that this economic downturn, like the previous ones, would also soon pass, Hoover stayed true to his principles and balked at the idea of direct government aid. In the case of the beleaguered farmers hit by a massive drought, the president instead led a successful fundraising campaign in conjunction with the Red Cross and raised $10 million for its relief fund. Yet when pressed by Congress to provide direct aid to the same farmers, he insisted that any legislation directed to do so should be limited to authorizing loans and not gifts; these were also to be limited to seed or fodder and not gifts or even human food.[5]

Then the wheels fell off the world's economy. Europe fell to the Depression, and England went off the gold standard. The prospect of the United States economy losing an outlet by which it could prop itself up from this economic dinge was too much even for Hoover to handle. By 1930, the dollar was left all but alone in the world of devalued currencies. This prompted a long raid on American stores of gold, whisking them away to Europe at a rate of $25 million a day.[6] Business could no longer help itself, let alone help the people—something that Hoover was hanging his hat on as a true believer in laissez-faire policies and government deregulation. It was at this point, nearly two years into the Depression, when the president shifted into high gear and proposed a sweeping number of reforms that would only be equaled— or perhaps imitated—by his successor's New Deal program. This was a new Hoover. A man still in control of his destiny. But was it too late?

By 1931, President Hoover's Reconstruction Finance Corporation proposed temporary government loans "to establish industries, railways, and financial institutions which [could not] otherwise secure credit, and where such advances [would] protect the credit structure and stimulate employment."[7] Most notably, the president authorized the construction of the Boulder Dam, which would later bear his name. In addition to providing electricity and a steady water supply to the area, it would also create hundreds if not thousands of much-needed jobs. Next came the Federal Home Loan Bank Act, lowering homeowners' mortgage rates and helping farmers keep their lands through refinancing options. And while some still believed that this new Hoover would turn things around, the 1930 congressional elections said otherwise. With the Republican majority in the Senate dropping down to one, the beleaguered party also lost control of the House of Representatives. It was now up to Hoover and the little pull that he still had with the American people to prove that he was the answer to their problems. Or at the very least, save the little respect he still held and turn around the ailing legacy he was about to leave behind. But then came the Bonus March. When it was over, there was no legacy left to save.

Led by Walter Waters, the Bonus Expeditionary Force came to the capital in the summer of 1932 to show their support for the Patman Bill under congressional consideration. Among other things, the bill would allow Congress to pay a monetary bonus to veterans of World War I ahead of schedule. The bonus was promised in 1924 when the legislative branch overrode Calvin Coolidge's veto of promising to

Taken in 1932, the image captures the squalid living conditions of the Bonus Marchers in one of the encampments in Washington D.C. (photograph by Underwood & Underwood, Library of Congress).

properly compensate veterans for their service through a bonus payment deferred to 1945. However, the money, roughly $500 per veteran, was needed now. As stated by LaFeber, "the veterans aroused considerable sympathy, but the Hoover administration believed the case against them to be overwhelming: payment of the bonus would wreck hopes for a balanced budget, give preferential treatment to veterans over other needy citizens, and entitle those veterans who were well-off to payment at a time of declining tax revenues."[8]

As the roughly 22,000 veterans, along with their families, camped out in a shantytown within sight of the Capitol in June of 1932, Hoover initially responded by providing food and supplies as a sign of respecting their right to a peaceful assembly. The police chief, Pelham D. Glassford, himself a veteran of the Great War, did the same. The House passed the supporting bill fairly quickly; it was now all up to the June 17 Senate vote. In the most shocking turn of events for the veterans—although all signs pointed to it in retrospect—the Senate rejected the bill by a large margin. After allocating $100,000 in early July to provide loans for any expenses the marchers might incur in their return journey home, Congress closed its doors for the summer session. Only 5,160 men took advantage of the offer, and the rest, having no home or jobs to return to, remained for a few more weeks.[9] Embarrassed and potentially afraid—Hoover thought most of the Bonus Marchers were communists and rabble-rousers—the president requested that the veterans and their families leave. While most trickled out of the capital throughout the month of July, thousands still remained hoping to sway Hoover to fight on their behalf. As the group was becoming agitated and quasi-violent, the Capitol Police and the National Guard marched into the "Hooverville" on the morning of July 28, 1932, to officially disband the Bonus Expeditionary Force.

* * * * * *

It was shortly after 12:30 in the afternoon that it dawned on Chief Pelham D. Glassford and the leaders of the Metropolitan Police as well as the commissioner that the situation was now out of local police hands. As reported weeks later in a 6,000-word report to the U.S. president by then-Attorney General William D. Mitchell, the entire police—leaving parts of the city completely unprotected—was called from their posts and assembled near the Hooverville shortly after news of the shooting spread through the crowd. And even at that point, they were outnumbered 15 to 1.[10] Managing to get himself out of the thick of things, Glassford got to the office of the district commissioner at 1:00 p.m. When asked about the status at the shantytown, he responded that the situation was no longer in his control and that the police could no longer hold the Bonus Marchers in check. It was then that he was asked the direct question: "Do you think it is necessary to secure the assistance of federal troops?" With dried blood on his face, the veteran of the Great War shook his head in the affirmative.

By 2:00 p.m., multiple squadrons of cavalry from Fort Myer, Virginia, rushed into D.C. and headed for the White House. As the situation near the Capitol was escalating, there was a general fear that the riot might move on to the presidential mansion and the president himself might be in danger. Brigadier General Miles had orders to clear the area between Third and Sixth streets and Pennsylvania Avenue and Missouri Avenue, a wide area, "using such force as might be necessary."[11] By the end of the day, the White House would be guarded by a combination of troops, machine gun units, and tanks. Meanwhile, the first of the army contingent to arrive at the scene of the camp riot was, fittingly, an army ambulance. This was followed around 2:30 p.m. by a bugle call and subsequent heavy trucks full of troops from Fort Washington rumbling up Pennsylvania Avenue. They were followed by heavy tanks and General Douglas MacArthur—a one-time war hero still 10 years from becoming one once again—in his official car.

The soldiers quickly dismounted from the army trucks and began clearing away the crowds of onlookers that packed the sidewalks. Then came the order to put on gas masks. Hurling tear bombs, the soldiers began clearing out the camp and buildings with bayonets pointed at all those who defied them. As MacArthur strode up and down the street barking orders, veterans began scrambling out of buildings and shacks, "their eyes smarting."[12] Within an hour and a half, the main camp was taken. "We'll make a clean job of it," stated the famous general whose soldiers continued routing the veterans and moving to the smaller adjacent offshoot camps. By then, the camps had gone up in flames—something that the army denied causing. As the shacks burned, MacArthur's army stood and watched the flames behind them illuminating the now dark sky. And then, "as though campaigning," they established a camp on the pavement and served "mess."[13]

It was not until after 9:00 p.m. when the troops began to move towards another camp across the capital. Determined to rid Washington, D.C., of all Bonus Army camps and not just the one near the Capitol, MacArthur moved his army—tanks, cavalry, and infantry—across the Anacostia Flats where thousands of veterans greeted them with boos and curse words. After sending a staff officer ahead to give the men in the camp one hour to evacuate all women and children, the troops were ready to move in. Then, when the hour was upon them, the soldiers were temporarily frozen in place. As if simultaneously and at different points throughout the entire camp, huts burst into flames. Not to be deterred, MacArthur ordered his men to put on their gas masks, fix bayonets, and enter the burning shantytown once more. The infantry advanced, driving back all those who remained. MacArthur retired and left General Miles in charge of mopping up any remnants of the Bonus Expeditionary Force's march on Washington.

---

10. The Unfortunate Bonus, July 28, 1932

As MacArthur sat in his car and received regular dispatches from the "front," the flames in the nearby camp, as well as those in the bigger and smaller sister camps across town, slowly ate away at the timber huts. In fact, the fires would rage for hours, forcing all six city fire companies to pool their resources in extinguishing them. Yet even at the moment the fires started, it was evident to all the troops on the ground that the Bonus Army had already left without putting up a fight. After all, if not they, who else would know that putting up a fight against the U.S. military was all but futile? Shortly after the reports of the camp being cleared out began coming in, General Miles stepped out of his vehicle, walked towards the flames, conferred with his staff officer, and, upon hearing his response, dispatched him to MacArthur with a message: mission fulfilled.[14] As one Pennsylvania newspaper put it, "the Battle of Washington had ended."[15]

Chased out of the capital, the quasi-army dispersed across the nation, many never returning home but simply continuing on the road towards finding jobs and new lives. Over the city from Anacostia at its extreme southeast border to the northern district line, "groups of veterans were seen, some trudging along on foot carrying blankets, frying pans, canteens and other camping equipment; some, more fortunate, riding in trucks or disreputable automobiles." The next day newspapers wrote of vets "[sitting] around the fringes of their former camps, just beyond the bayonet points of the infantrymen on guard, and contemplating the ruins of what had been their homes for two months, some sullenly and with resentment, others in philosophical or even humorous mood."[16] As police directed traffic out of the capital city, they were greeted with the sight of ramshackle motorcars and trucks of Bonus Marchers solemnly making their exodus to parts unknown. One veteran from Virginia, his little daughter beside him, sat on the railroad tracks overlooking the charred remnants of the camp. He refused to budge when prompted by a policeman. "When you enlist in the army," he kept repeating, "you enlist to protect your country, not to fight against it."[17]

Within days, Attorney General Mitchell cited the identification of Communists within the Bonus Expeditionary Force as the impetus for the necessity of federal involvement in disbanding the Bonus Army: "There is irrefutable proof that a very large body of Communists and radicals, some ex-servicemen and some not, were in the city, as part of the Bonus Army, circulating among them and working diligently to incite them to disorder."[18] President Hoover himself made a statement: "The investigation has been completed ... which shows the character of many of the persons assembled [as communists and rabble-rousers]." To quell some of the negative attention he was anticipating, Hoover was quick to add, "I wish to state empathetically that the extraordinary portion of criminal, Communist and non-veteran elements amongst the marchers, as shown by this report, should not be taken to reflect upon the many thousands of honest, law-abiding men who came to Washington with full right of presentation of their views to Congress."[19] Even Hoover should have known that the racket was up. There were nearly five months left until the next presidential election. But Hoover had already lost.

* * * * * *

President Herbert Hoover's actions of late July 1932, where he sent in the military to forcibly remove what the nation perceived to be the real national heroes now starving and in need of help, had only confirmed what many already believed. The people's president was heartless. It would not have mattered if the Democrats ran Mickey Mouse against him in the upcoming election. He would not win. In fact, it would be nearly three decades before a Republican president would sit in the Oval Office again. Yet, all of this was in the future. Herbert Hoover still needed to survive his last few months as the president of the United States.

"The blood of these hungry men is on his hands!" stated Texas Congressman Wright Patman. "I cannot understand why the army was used to drive the men from Washington who were not in government buildings but in homes they had built with their own hands," he added.[20] Another congressman, Senator Black from Alabama, criticized the president for the use of troops "without justification in fact, theory, or law."[21] The National Committee for the Defense of Political Prisoners sent a telegram to the White House calling the dispersal of the Washington Bonus Army an act of "callous barbarism."[22] One Washington resident went as far as writing an editorial letter in the *Washington Daily News* stating, "I voted for Herbert Hoover in 1928.... God forgive me and keep me alive, at least until the polls open!"[23]

It was not just the domestic press that tore into President Hoover.

The events of late July made their way across the pond and were often sarcastically covered by major European newspapers. An editorial in the French *Le Journal* spoke of street charges, fusillades, tank patrols, and gas attacks, which the writer said took place not in poor, upset Europe but in the America that is "so proud of giving an example of order." The paper went on to ask what would have happened if the soldiers did not have gas, tanks, and "all that apparatus which Americans [stigmatize], but which they know well how to use when it becomes necessary."[24] Perhaps ironically, the front pages of German newspapers placed the Washington riots front and center next to stories of the important Reichstag elections that were being held a few days hence—elections that would eventually see one Adolf Hitler elected chancellor of Germany. The German paper *Mittag Zeitung* printed two columns worth of information, ending with a paragraph titled "Hoover's End." The article went on to say that the president's chances for re-election had been "killed by the brutal evacuation of the veterans."[25] Only London's *The Evening News* somewhat sided with Hoover, albeit in a brazen way: "The lesson is unfortunate, but the moral is plain," the paper said. "A show of arms can and usually does secure peace."[26]

On July 29, 1932, the day when most newspapers vilified Herbert Hoover, Franklin Delano Roosevelt, with the *New York Times* spread out in front of him, phoned his friend and aide, Felix Frankfurter. "Well, Felix," he said, "this will elect me."[27] He was not wrong. For months leading up to the election in November, movie theaters throughout the nation showed newsreels of the Bonus Army's eviction to collective boos and curses coming from the audience. As far as the American people were concerned, their leader was not compassionate, even heartless, and borderline cruel.

It would be a stretch to say that Herbert Hoover had much of a chance of winning the presidency of the United States in 1932, yet the same was once said of Harry Truman running against Thomas Dewey in 1948, or more recently Donald J. Trump topping Hillary Clinton to clinch the presidency in 2016. It was not until the Bonus Army debacle that Hoover completely lost his support among the American people. Up to that point, his Democratic opponent led a very cautious campaign, promising a New Deal for the American people without ever really providing any specifics of what precisely that deal would entail. Roosevelt knew that he could not afford to trip up, lest that distract the people from Hoover's failing policies. In fact, "FDR spoke in such generalities and exuded so much optimism that some commentators wondered if he understood the extraordinary challenges facing the nation."[28] It was not until the Bonus Army exodus in the late summer of 1932 that FDR felt comfortable speaking up and being more direct with his message. After all, he really did not have anything to lose. Outlining his New Deal philosophy in a September campaign speech, the would-be-president stated that the federal government needed to assume responsibility for the welfare of the nation—a direct counter-argument to his opponent.

As for Hoover, the remainder of his campaigning could not have gone any worse either. The president was heckled at nearly every stop by hostile crowds as foodstuffs pelted his motorcades. It came as no surprise when, come November, FDR won with 22.8 million votes to Hoover's 15.7 million in an election that marked a turning point in American politics.[29] The result of Hoover's failure and the subsequent election of Franklin D. Roosevelt signaled the emergence of a Democratic coalition that would shape national politics for the next four decades. As stated by historian James A. Henretta, "Roosevelt won the support of the Solid South, which returned to the Democratic fold; and he drew substantial support in the West and in the cities showing Democrats now appealed to immigrants and urban ethnic groups."[30] However, not shown by the statistics was the fact that many people did not vote *for* Roosevelt as much as *against* Herbert Clark Hoover. One wonders what destiny history held for Hoover had an immigrant and one-time U.S. soldier William Hushka not been killed by a bullet fired by a frightened police officer. Would the police have been able to contain the Bonus Expeditionary Force? Would they be compelled to ask for federal assistance had a police officer not shot a man who sacrificed so much for his nation only to be rejected by it in his most considerable time of need? As is often the case in such matters, what-if questions do not change the past but only show us the potential for a different future.

For Further Reading

There are many great newspaper articles detailing the events available online from the newspapers.com service, but if one does not have the needed access, a trip to the library can be more than rewarding. While there are, surprisingly, few books written on the topic of the

Bonus Army, there are enough to do the topic justice. There is *B.E.F.: The Whole Story of the Bonus March* (2010) by Walter W. Walters, which contains a firsthand account of the proceedings. There is also the short (but still all-encompassing and well-researched) *The Bonus Army: An American Epic* (2004) by Paul Dickson and Thomas B. Allen. Of interest would also be Kenneth Whyte's *Hoover: An Extraordinary Life in Extraordinary Times* (2017) and Charles Rappleye's *Herbert Hoover in the White House: The Ordeal of the Presidency* (2016). Both books examine the president's reliance on the idea of "rugged individualism" and perhaps the reasoning behind his actions with relation to the Bonus March. As for the continuation of the story of the American "Doughboys" and what happened to them after the end of the Great War, there is no better book than Richard Rubin's *The Last of the Doughboys: The Forgotten Generation and Their Forgotten World War* (2013), which sees the author track down and interview all living World War I veterans at the start of the twenty-first century.

11

Machine Gun Challenge
to Uncle Sam,
June 17, 1933

The Missouri Pacific train carrying three Bureau of Investigation (BOI) agents and their captive arrived at the Kansas City Union Station in Missouri right on time at 7:15 a.m. The tallest of the three agents left his colleagues behind and made his way to the loading platform to meet with two additional agents and two uniformed police officers requested to assist with the prisoner transfer. Informed that the surrounding area had been checked for anything suspicious and all appeared clear and ready to go, the agents and officers went back to the train to get their prisoner.

Seven men armed with shotguns and revolvers escorted one of the most successful bank robbers in American history, Frank Nash, to the two unmarked Chevrolets parked right outside the station. The tallest agent, Francis Joseph Lackey, clearly in charge of the operation, ordered Nash to sit in the front as he and two other agents got in the back. Nobody noticed a green Plymouth parked a few yards to the side—not until three men ran out of it with machine guns. "Let 'em have it!"[1] A fatal bullet struck Kansas City police officer Grooms, and then another one hit Officer Hermanson. As both fell to the ground, another agent hiding behind the driver's side door collapsed with a mortal head wound, and one more was thrown to the ground. More bullets ripped into the three officers sitting in the back of the car. One of the attackers stepped over a wounded agent and opened the car door, now riddled with bullet holes. No use: the man they came to spring was dead in the front seat. The men did not wait to hear the screams from crying women and children echoing throughout the station.

* * * * *

The event at Union Station lasted 30 seconds. Before speeding away from the scene, the murderers' machine gun bullets killed Nash—albeit accidentally—and four officers of the law. The instant the first bullet entered into Officer W.J. Grooms's chest, the matter took on a new level of urgency for the media and the federal government. Robbing banks and killing fellow criminals was one thing, but cold-blooded murder of lawmen in broad daylight was another.

The event, dubbed the Kansas City Massacre by the press, would signal the turning point in the U.S. government's fight against organized crime. Labeled as "a brazen challenge to the federal government on the part of the underworld" by the Associated Press in 1933, the event directly contributed to creating the modern Federal Bureau of Investigation.[2] Yet, perhaps more importantly, it led to the ascendance to prominence of one of the most powerful men in twentieth-century America, J. Edgar Hoover. Finally, given the resources needed to fight crime after the shooting and killing of five officers in Missouri, Hoover used the event as a springboard to complete his reshaping of the bureau into a force—one that, according to historian David Gramm, "during his nearly five-decade reign as director, he would deploy not only to combat crime but also to commit egregious abuses of power."[3]

Before the Kansas City Massacre of 1933, the Bureau of Investigation (BOI)—as the agency was known before being renamed the Federal Bureau of Investigation in 1935—was amidst a badly needed house cleaning of sorts. Established in 1908, by 1921, when young lawyer J. Edgar Hoover was named assistant director, the BOI had only a few hundred agents and a handful of offices. Most importantly, its jurisdiction over crimes was severely limited by undefined and legislative decrees. Instead of major crimes at the state level, the agents handled investigative work relating to cases that crossed state lines, such as antitrust and banking violations, interstate car heists, contraceptives, escapes by federal prisoners, and crimes committed on Indian reservations.[4] While some agents, many former private detectives, were corrupt and took bribes, others were proud of the political connections that garnered them the appointments. Without any real authority over real cases and without any adequately trained and qualified personnel, the BOI was what one congressman at the time called a "bureaucratic bastard."[5]

Ironically, even at the time of the 1933 massacre, federal agents were still not allowed to carry firearms or make arrests, for which they had to call a local law officer. The guns that Lackey and his fellow agents carried during the massacre were their own and technically not allowed. The events in Kansas City would ensure that it would be the last time bureau agents would be shackled with such legislative restrictions.

Quickly rising through the ranks, the now 29-year-old Hoover took over as director in 1924, determined to give some credence to the federal institution. Firing crooks and incompetent agents, the new director instituted a new code of conduct for his employees. There was no more drinking on the job and regular inspections of field operations. He also weeded out those unqualified for the job, taking the bureau from 650 agents in 1924 to just 339 by the end of the decade.[6] With the newly rigorous hiring criteria, background checks, and formal training, the men representing the BOI were finally professional and organized to be effective. By the time of the events of June 1933, Hoover had instituted uniform crime reports, constructed a modern criminal laboratory, started a training academy for his agents, and assembled a national fingerprint file.[7] This last accomplishment brought the bureau to a certain scientific standard that Hoover aspired to in order to modernize law enforcement across the nation. Prints from all police agencies around the U.S. were consolidated under the guidance of the BOI's Identification Division, allowing for the ability to more quickly and accurately identify criminals.

Yet, as a crime wave spurred on by Prohibition and bootlegging gangsters reached its peak in the late 1920s, the BOI was still nothing more than an investigative agency without much power to counter crime. By the time Prohibition was repealed in 1933 and organized crime subsided, the Great Depression created a new type of criminal. Spurred on by the bleak existence in the biggest economic downturn in the nation's history, rural criminals, far removed from big-city gangs and organized crime, brought the excitement of real-life Hollywood drama to the starving masses. The public, caught up in the Robin Hood lore associated with these crimes, which mostly revolved around bank robberies in the Midwest, tended to turn a blind eye to the fact that they were killers. The press further fueled this lore by giving these criminals creative names like Frank "Jelly" Nash, or "Baby Face" Nelson, or George "Machine Gun" Kelly.

Looking at them from a distance, these criminals gave off the perception of robbing the rich to share with the poor—although no real sharing ever took place. Still, when Baby Face Nelson would rob a bank, he would claim loan and mortgage records as readily as he did all the cash. Considering the Great Depression and the thousands of homes, farms, and businesses foreclosed by the banks, especially in the Midwest, it is not hard to see why many people believed these criminals to be national heroes.[8] The arrest of Frank Nash came directly out of this midwestern crime wave, which dominated the news from 1933 until 1934, when it ended. Most of the crimes occurred in just a handful of states: Missouri, Iowa, Indiana, Illinois, Wisconsin, Minnesota, and Ohio. Yet, the colorful characters and the often helpless law enforcement without proper training and hindered by the fact that their jurisdictions stopped at their borders dominated national news. And although different from the big-city gangsters of the 1920s, these Depression-era criminals were no less dangerous.

The hunt for the criminals who would all become known as "public enemies" was in full swing nationwide, albeit without much BOI involvement as the crimes committed did not necessarily violate federal laws. This would change slightly after the infamous kidnapping and death of the baby of nationally renowned aviator Charles Lindbergh in 1932, which led to the federal government extending some jurisdiction into state crimes of national stature to the BOI. Still outgunned and without any right to make arrests, the bureau's agents began assisting local authorities with their war on crime. This was how agents F.J. Lackey and Raymond J. Caffrey found themselves in Kansas City on that June morning—spurring on the evolution of the BOI into the Federal Bureau of Investigation and ushering in the dominion of one Edgar J. Hoover.

* * * * * *

Frank Nash, a famed midwestern criminal, made a name for himself through numerous bank robberies, murders, and a successful 1930 prison break from the federal penitentiary at Fort Leavenworth in Kansas, where he had been serving a 25-year sentence since 1924. When a tip was reported to the bureau that the escaped convict had crossed state or even national lines—one tipoff had him hiding in Canada—the search for the elusive criminal began in earnest. And although the BOI still could not carry out arrests, its new methods—relying on crime

A young J. Edgar Hoover at the height of his popularity following the successful crusade against the midwestern crime spree and prior to the United States entrance into World War II. Picture taken in 1940 (photograph by Harris & Ewing, Library of Congress).

scene photography, lab work, handwriting analysis, etc.—implemented by J. Edgar Hoover had at the least strengthened their reputation as solid investigators.

11. Machine Gun Challenge to Uncle Sam, June 17, 1933

The bureau actually completed Nash's résumé when they were able to tie him to further robberies and the December 1931 escape of seven prisoners from the same penitentiary that he'd vacated the year prior. After helping apprehend his one-time conspirators, the investigators learned that Nash was holding out with a fake mustache, a toupee, and a new girlfriend in Hot Springs, Arkansas, considered at the time to be a gamblers' safe heaven. It was the largest operation of its kind in the nation with 10 major casinos, numerous smaller house spinoffs, off-track booking for horse races, and prostitution rings.[9] Among many things, it was an excellent microcosm and a glaring example of local and state law enforcement's inability to fight crime. Even by 1937, when a sheriff attempted to enforce the state's anti-gambling laws and secure honest elections, he was found murdered.

Unable to stay unnoticed for too long, Nash resurfaced with his new girlfriend in Hot Springs in 1932. Two Bureau of Investigation agents stationed in Oklahoma, Joe Lackey and Frank Smith, were ordered to apprehend the escaped convict and escort him back to prison, which proved easier than anticipated. The fake facial hair and wig did not do a good enough job for a man who fancied himself the center of attention. Nash was drinking beer at one of the area's speakeasies—it would be nearly a year before President Roosevelt would repeal the Eighteenth Amendment and do away with the temperance law—when the bureau's agents identified him. Because they were "only BOI agents," they could not carry out the arrest themselves and needed the assistance of the police chief of McAlester, Oklahoma, Otto Reed. As per a later report, Nash's wife telephoned her husband's old accomplices and informed them of the agents' traveling plans and final destination—which she happened to overhear. As the three men and their prisoner boarded a train for Kansas City, Missouri, and Nash's eventual trip back to Fort Leavenworth, a plan was already being put in place to spring him.

According to newspapers reports, the morning of Saturday, June 17, 1933, was a cool one at Union Railway Station in Kansas City, Missouri. Everything seemed orderly as the latest train arrived without much fanfare. The popular Harvey restaurant was busy preparing breakfast orders. With its grand arches and uniformed attendants, the lobby echoed the clicking heels of women in summery white dresses accompanying their young children.[10] As a tremendous noise came in from the outside, many disregarded it as potential car exhausts backfiring, but then a white-faced woman rushed into the great hall. "Men killed outside!" she screamed.[11] As some men and women ran for the doors to see the commotion outside; others grabbed their children's hands and ran for cover.

Nash's train had arrived at the station roughly 10 minutes earlier. Dispatched to meet him and his accompanying officers were two Kansas City detectives, Hermanson and Grooms, Kansas City Special Agent R.E. Vetterli, and another BOI agent, Raymond J. Caffrey. Only Vetterli, Smith, and Lackey would live past the next quarter of an hour, Lackey with three bullets in his back. When the train arrived slightly before 7:15 a.m., Agent Lackey wasted no time finding Vetterli on the platform. The two discussed the location of the two vehicles parked directly outside and the route they would take to transfer the handcuffed Nash. It was time.

Mrs. Lottie West, a caseworker with the Travelers Aid station, looked up just in time to see the group of seven officers take a handcuffed Nash through the doors from the trains and then march him across the lobby. She quickly noticed that two of the officers were carrying sawed-off shotguns and another kept his hand at his hip, ready to draw his revolver. The group crossed the station in a pack, with Nash in the middle. "He must be pretty bad," Mrs. West remarked to a friend from the station dining room.[12] With her curiosity piqued, she left her desk, followed the group out onto the station platform, and watched them cross the street to two parked cars. She would later recall seeing a big man coming out from behind another vehicle and opening fire. And then she was on the floor, her hands covering her head. Before she could say anything, another woman ran into the station screaming that men were being killed outside.

After walking escorted through the station, Nash was directed to the nearest of the two cars. As he attempted to get in the back, he was stopped and told he would be riding in the front. Before climbing into the car, the officers glanced around the parking lot, and, once more agreeing that all looked clear, Lackey gently pushed Nash's head down to guide him into the front seat. The detective then opened the back door and sat directly behind his prisoner, with Smith and Reed getting in on the other side of him. Caffrey was chosen as the driver and was opening the car door to get in when the commotion started. The two Kansas police detectives stood near the front of the car watching the proceedings as Vetterli began walking to his car when he heard, "Put 'em up. Up! Up!"

"I looked up and saw a man with a machine gun blazing away from near the southeast corner of the car," testified a shaken-up Vetterli later that day, himself wounded by the shooting. He fell to the ground after a shot hit his arm. "Hermanson and Grooms fell to the pavement in front of me, their bodies riddled. The windshield of Caffrey's car was splintering, and the men inside it were powerless from the red fire from the machine gun," recalled the special agent.[13] Other witnesses would testify to seeing one big man and two smaller men "carrying one of these guns with a cylinder on top of it and shooting right at the officers."[14] Nearby stood six Catholic sisters, frozen in place and unable to move lest they be hit by the flying bullets shattering windows in the nearby building. One of the killers ran up to the police car and looked inside. Seeing Nash's bloody body slumped over the dashboard, he yelled something back to the other men who were already getting back into their green Plymouth parked nearby. A motorcycle patrolman assigned to the station, M.K. Fanning, ran to the scene and began firing at the car that sped away and quickly disappeared around the corner.

A tragic picture met the men and women who ran from inside the station to see the commotion. The Chevrolet was riddled with bullets. The shattered glass seemed to be everywhere on the pavement, including on top of the bodies of the two police officers whose faces were unrecognizable through the multiple bullet wounds. Caffrey's body lay near the driver's side door; Agent Vetterli lay moaning near the other vehicle. In the middle of the Chevrolet's back seat, Agent Smith had slumped down when the shooting started; the only one to come out of the ordeal unscathed, he felt his friend Reed slump down on him. Now that all was quiet, he looked up and saw that Nash had been hit. "Agent Lackey began to groan. I put my arm under Ott Reed's [slumping] head and tried to comfort Lackey," Smith would recall. "I noticed that Lackey's revolver handle had been splintered by a bullet. Maybe that was why he wasn't killed outright like the others. Maybe the bullet ricocheted."[15]

This was no Saint Valentine's Day Massacre where gangsters killed other gangsters. This was a cold-blooded killing of officers of the law. To J. Edgar Hoover, the director of the Bureau of Investigation, this arrogant disregard for authority was nothing less than "a challenge to law and order and civilization itself."[16] The bureau wasted no time in investigating the perpetrators. It was soon on the tail of Vernon C. Miller, Adam Richetti, and Charles "Pretty Boy" Floyd, whom they identified as the prime suspects.[17] Still, to the public and Hoover, apprehension of just three men would not be enough. It was time for a war against crime, and it would be the new and improved Bureau of Investigation, soon calling itself the Federal Bureau of Investigation, that would lead the way.

* * * * *

The effects of the first bullet (and the countless others that followed) that struck down the officers at Kansas City's Union Station on June 17, 1933, could be seen as twofold. First, it liberated the BOI from the bureaucratic legislation that kept it from becoming a significant police force, allowing it to end the Midwest crime wave within a year of its beginning. Doing so also eliminated potential copycats and changed the public's perception of the criminals as the good guys. Subsequently, the second effect was popularizing J. Edgar Hoover and his agency, now renamed the Federal Bureau of Investigation. The federal agents, or "G-men" as the public now called them, graced the covers of comic books, magazines, and movie posters. There was no longer any doubt as to who was the criminal and who the hero. This last consequence also led to the rise of one of the most powerful men in American history, J. Edgar Hoover, which in itself left a lasting legacy.

The Kansas City Massacre, as the newspapers dubbed it, at long last tore down any remnants of opposition to extending the power and reach of the federal government in keeping people safe against crime. These would no longer be strictly local and state cases, but, when applicable, federal ones. And according to at least one paper of the time, the criminals themselves were to blame. "For the wave of public indignation against organized criminals which awakened the nation from the lethargy of years, brought the law enforcement agencies of Uncle Sam into the picture, and ultimately put crime on the run, the underworld can blame its most daring deed ... the Kansas City Union Station massacre of last June 17," proclaimed the *Reading Times* of Pennsylvania.[18]

A month after the tragic event, J. Edgar Hoover stood behind the podium at the International Association of Chiefs of Police and asked the police forces across the nation to join him in a national war on crime. "Those who participated in this cold-blooded murder will be hunted down," Hoover promised to loud applause. "Sooner or later, the penalty which is their due will be paid."[19] Together with Attorney General Homer Cummings, the director of the BOI used the public outcry to push through Congress a sweeping reform bill that would, for lack of a better word, unleash the bureau on America's vices. Using the pretense that crime had gotten out of hand across the entire United States and that many of the states were unable, through lack of funds, training, etc. to control it, the federal governments would step in to fill the needed gaps. Within months of the massacre, Congress passed a collection of new major crime bills—interestingly, almost without any opposition from the states, which usually valued their political autonomy regarding legislative jurisdiction.

Enacted in 1934, the statutes known as Crime Control Acts included provisions for punishment for killing and assaulting federal officers, extortion, transportation of kidnapped persons, and interstate flight, as well as provisions defining crimes in connection with the administration of federal prisons and crimes committed against banks operating under the laws of the United States.[20] The effect was once again twofold. The new rules gave the parameters of what constituted a federal crime and granted the BOI new powers in enforcing them. The bureau's agents were allowed to issue warrants, make arrests, and carry weapons for the first time. As they would no longer be mere investigators, Hoover expanded the agency by hiring former police officers for proper police training. It was time to wage war.

The most famous Midwest criminals were labeled "public enemies" and hunted down across the country. Altogether, it took the new BOI a calendar year, from 1933 to 1944, to end the midwestern crime wave and change the paradigm of the so-called good criminal. First, after the passage of the 1934 Crime Control Acts in May of that year, came the downfall of the infamous crime couple Bonnie and Clyde, known for robbing banks and killing innocent bystanders. And although the final credit would ultimately go to a pair of Texas lawmen, the BOI investigation proved essential in the apprehension—or rather entrapment, as the two were stopped on the road and killed by the officers. A few months later, in July, the BOI, this time on their own, shot and killed the bank robber and murderer labeled "Public Enemy Number One," John Dillinger. "Organized society has triumphed, as it must, over one who would defy its laws," said William Stanley, assistant attorney general, the day after Dillinger's killing by the bureau's agents.[21]

Dillinger's takedown is further significant in that it also gave us the first real inkling of the type of man J. Edgar Hoover was, and hence, the kind of agency his bureau would become for nearly another 40 years. When Melvin Purvis, a special agent stationed in Chicago, was paraded through the media—accurately—as the man responsible for planning and finally catching the criminal, Hoover was quick to relegate the man to a desk job and eventually force his resignation. The credit should have belonged to him and his BOI, thought the director, and not any one man. Newspapers were soon fed a new version of events. Each time Purvis made the paper, Hoover made sure to say that this was the bureau's victory—hence his as its director. He even went as far as naming another agent as the one more responsible— anything to discredit the man who was becoming a media darling. By August, *American Detective Magazine* quoted one of the agents present the night of Dillinger's shooting, giving credit where at least one man thought it was due: "One man alone is responsible for the end of John Dillinger, and that man is J. Edgar Hoover."[22] When Purvis resigned from the bureau amidst the spat with his boss, Hoover told the media that he was fired for laziness and showboating.

Working the public, Hoover sanctioned a new tell-all radio series titled *G-Men*—a nickname for government agents supposedly given to them by gangster George "Machine Gun" Kelly. In this new version of events, Purvis's role was not even mentioned. Hoover's face was soon staring at young kids from cereal boxes, comic strips, and toys, telling them of the brave exploits of his G-Men, all faceless yet courageous. And although, as far as the public was concerned, no G-Man stood out or had a real name, the same could not be said for the director, who proudly represented his bureau. There was no limit to the BOI's self-glorification. By 1935 there were even Hollywood movies, where the director's image yet again took center stage. The poster for the Hollywood-produced documentary film *You Can't Get Away with It*, from Universal, said it best: "The First Authentic Picture of Hoover, Himself, and His G-Men, Behind the Scenes and in Action!"[23]

When Purvis published his version of events—describing his role in receiving a tipoff where Dillinger was going to be, organizing the bust, and being the one to identify Dillinger and lead to his killing—he was quickly discredited by Hoover as attention-seeking and dishonest. After all, Hoover was the man the public now knew and recognized. The bureau was Hoover's show and nobody else's. As for Purvis, his life was ruined. It seemed that no matter where he went or what job he applied for, Hoover got there first with private warnings that Purvis was unreliable.[24] As it became apparent that the director's wrath would never end, Purvis took out his former BOI revolver and killed himself. For historians, the story of Dillinger, Purvis, and Hoover from 1934 to 1935 marks the first apparent case of Hoover's paranoia, foreshadowing the lengths he was willing to go to stay in power. And the lengths he was willing to push the bureau to do so.

As for avenging the Kansas City Massacre, the BOI apprehended and killed the man it believed responsible for its organization in October 1934. Charles "Pretty Boy" Floyd was finally cornered and killed by the bureau while resisting arrest. Of his two accomplices in the shootout at Union Station, one's body was found a ditch outside of Detroit from an apparent mob hit. The other was apprehended, arrested, and executed two years after standing trial in 1935. As one historian put it, "the days of the small Bureau were over."[25] Fittingly, the federal government and J. Edgar Hoover christened the re-birth and new identity of the agency with a new name in 1935: the Federal Bureau of Investigation (FBI). The name and the times of the pencil-pushing investigative force unable to carry out the arrest of Frank Nash on the eve of the Kansas City Massacre would no longer exist. It would be the FBI that would complete the full sweep of rounding up the midwestern criminals with the 1935 apprehension of Alvin Karpis and his Barker brother sidekicks known for robbing banks and trains and engineering two major kidnappings of wealthy Minnesota business executives in 1933.[26]

As the Great Depression and crime waves of the 1930s turned into World War II, Hoover's FBI turned its attention to gathering and compiling millions of files on unsuspecting Americans whom the director saw as subversive. It would continue its spying on the population suspected of communist affiliation during the Red Scare of the 1950s and then work to disturb any radical organization that sprang up in the 1960s. And while it used its power to infiltrate, monitor, and disrupt dangerous groups such as the Ku Klux Klan, the FBI did the same with the civil rights and anti-war movements that characterized the decade.[27] The paranoia and determination the director of the FBI showed in going

Forfeited guns gathered by the police in the early 1900s at the time when many cities began to organize their police departments into functioning units with the impetus to curb crime (George Grantham Bain Collection, Library of Congress).

after Purvis, who he believed upstaged him in the months after the Kansas City Massacre, was a precursor to what the man would be capable of with a stronger bureau under his command.

When he died in 1972, J. Edgar Hoover had already compiled secret files on Martin Luther King, Jr., Eleanor Roosevelt, Muhammad Ali, and even Robert and John F. Kennedy, among countless others. He would allegedly use the often incriminating evidence—as was the case with JFK's extramarital affairs—to force his way into American politics. He infamously checkmated his new boss, Attorney General Robert Kennedy, when the young Kennedy wanted to fire him. After being told that not going along with Hoover's FBI or dismissing Hoover might prove embarrassing to his brother, RFK backed down. By the time Hoover served under his eighth president in 1969, the media and the public grew suspicious of the FBI's power and its director.[28] J. Edgar Hoover died in 1972, just as the investigation into the Watergate scandal that would lead to President Richard Nixon's resignation two years later began to unravel. The scope of the FBI's abuses of power since the 1930s finally came to light, and Congress thoroughly investigated the agency for its unconstitutional actions and surveillance.

Who is to say that the BOI and Hoover would never have amassed such power as they were granted after the machine gun bullets tore into officers of the law in June of 1933? Yet, it would be equally hard to argue that the Crime Control Acts, which came directly as a response to the public outcry that followed the Kansas City Massacre, gave the BOI and its director a blank check to expand their agency. Without that first bullet on June 17, 1933, and the hundreds that followed moments later, history most certainly would have seen a continuation of the midwestern crime wave. Hoover would remain as nothing but a young hotshot director of a bureaucratic agency that not many Americans knew existed. And the FBI, the extent of whose abuses and meddling throughout American history is still not fully understood—as is perhaps their positive impact in many other cases, to be fair—would still be nothing but a glorified yet powerless investigative agency.

For Further Reading

Curt Gentry's *J. Edgar Hoover: The Man and the Secrets* (Norton, 1991) is a great start for an all-encompassing and detailed history on Hoover's rise in the FBI. For the history of the bureau, Tim Weiner, a winner of a Pulitzer Prize, serves up a perfect overview in *Enemies: A History of the FBI* (2012). Weiner's account is very lively as well as informational, providing a fast-paced yet comprehensive look at the FBI from its early beginning as simply the Bureau of Investigation all the way up to the twenty-first century. For a more sensational look at Hoover's life and abuses of power, Marc Aronson's *Master of Deceit* (2021) does a good job picking out the rumors, which he intertwines with factual information. A little less formal and with a decent number of images, the book is nonetheless a great introduction to the infamous side of Hoover. And although not about the events described in this chapter, David Grann's *Killers of the Flower Moon: The Osage Murders and the Birth of the FBI* (2017) is an amazing story itself, but for this purpose, it also provides a great narrative about the early rise of Hoover and the FBI though a detailed character study.

12

A Catalyst for Change,
February 18, 1965

The Reverend C.T. Vivian had just finished speaking. People—around 600 men, women, and children—started for the door of the Zion United Methodist Church. They were there in this little church for a reason. It was located just one block away from the Perry County Jail. That night, they would stage a peaceful march up the road to protest the unlawful arrest of one of their own, civil rights worker James Orange. He had been arrested for his part in the "right to vote" campaign raging across the South. A 26-year-old, Jimmie Lee Jackson, grabbed his teenage sister's hand. He smiled and reassured her that everything was going to be okay. Behind them were Jimmie's mother and grandfather. They were some of the first people to step out of the church that night. The streetlights that normally illuminated the block were all turned off. It was pitch dark as he and his family stepped down the stairs. In the darkness ahead of him and his 600 brothers and sisters exiting the church were the local police force and 50 state troopers.

There were about 100 people out of the church when Police Chief T.O. Harris's booming voice broke the silence through an electric loudspeaker: "You are going to be arrested if you don't disperse. Go back to the church."[1] Yet for many of the marchers, the path was blocked. Some people had already made it to the street, while others were still pushing forward from the church and down the stairs. They began praying. Their voices drowned out Harris as he continued screaming into his loudspeaker. Then the troops moved in. And suddenly, still engulfed in darkness, Jimmie and his family were surrounded by screams, cries, and shouting. "Move! Move!" yelled the policemen as they pushed the people back into the church. Jackson saw clubs flashing through the darkness as they went up before coming down and striking women and children.

He needed to get his sister, mother, and grandfather out of there, and fast.

As people were forcibly pushed back up the stairs into the church, a small group of young black men ran away towards a side street. A local policeman sprinted after them. "Stop...!" Jackson saw an advantage. Still holding his sister's hand and now grabbing for his mother's, Jackson spurred on his grandfather and directed his family towards Mack's Café, directly behind the church. They passed a woman kneeling to pray on the pavement just as another officer slammed her face down into the concrete. Police clubs quickly fell on her ribs as she burst into sobbing moans.[2] A bottle sailed over their heads and towards the police who chased them. Jimmie managed to enter the restaurant's kitchen before the officers caught up to him. His head was clubbed almost instantly. From the floor, he saw his mother—who tried to protect him—receive the same treatment. Before he could get up under his own strength, he was dragged up and thrown across the room into a cigarette machine.

Wanting to help his mother, Jackson staggered forward. His eyesight distorted, he scanned the room, searching. He could hear his mother crying as she was being struck. Moving forward, he was suddenly thrown back. This time it was a bullet in his stomach that pinned him to the cigarette machine. Then another. "Who got him?!" a voice called out. "I got him," said Trooper James B. Fowler.[3] Bleeding profusely, Jackson stumbled out of the restaurant. Blood flowed through his hands as they shielded him from more blows coming from the police officer who followed him outside. He closed his eyes, and the world went dark.

* * * * * *

It would be an understatement to say that the struggle for the civil rights of African Americans intensified in the 1960s. The decade's efforts amounted to "the" civil rights movement. The short-term causes of the movement can be traced to the sympathetic and self-professed racist President Harry S. Truman. Moved by the horrific attacks on black servicemen returning from World War II, the 33rd commander-in-chief established the President's Committee on Civil Rights to uncover and report the rabid racism in the Deep South. With the proof he was seeking now in hand, in 1947, he urged Congress to pass legislation to combat it. While unable to get much past southern legislators, he did use his executive power to take the first step of the twentieth century towards equal rights among the races in desegregating the armed forces. Most importantly, he put the total moral weight of the presidency behind the struggle for civil rights, which would only encourage further activism.[4]

The National Association for the Advancement of Colored People (NAACP) reached its zenith in the 1950s after battling segregation in American courts since 1909. The case that is often pointed to as the birth of the modern civil rights movement was the association's victory in the Brown v. Board of Education court case of 1954, which de-segregated the American school system. And although the acceptance of the Brown ruling varied throughout the nation, President Dwight D. Eisenhower—who ironically also considered himself a racist—upheld and enforced the court's decision throughout the 1950s by protecting black students attending desegregated schools. The vital case was followed by the Montgomery bus boycott, which introduced the world to a seamstress and a young reverend who would become the face of the movement to entirely end segregation based on race and create an all-inclusive society. The boycott of the Montgomery public bussing system organized by Dr. Martin Luther King Jr. and spurred on by a single moment of Rosa Park's defiance in refusing to give up her seat to a white man on a bus, demonstrated the power of the black community when using direct but non-violent protest.

In 1957, one year following the bus boycott, President Eisenhower, acting perhaps more so on the idea of strengthening his black vote in the election of 1956, introduced to Congress the 1957 Civil Rights Act. At the time, only 20 percent of all southern African Americans were registered to participate in the next election. In one of his speeches, the president expressed his disbelief that only 7,000 of Mississippi's 900,000 blacks were allowed to vote and that the registrars were posing such impossible questions as "how many bubbles are there in a bar of soap?"[5] Still, by the time the bill made it through a Democratic Congress, it was but a shadow of its former self and did very little to help African Americans gain the right to vote. It was a case of déjà vu when the president pushed his 1960 Civil Rights Act through Congress a couple of years later.

During the presidency of John F. Kennedy, the civil rights

movement went through some of its brutal years with concurrent successes and highlights pushing the federal government to pass the most comprehensive civil rights legislation since perhaps Reconstruction in the 1860s. Following the Montgomery bus boycott, MLK set up the Southern Christian Leadership Conference (SCLC) and, together with the NAACP and the Student Non-Violent Coordinating Committee (SNCC), organized the movement. During this time in the early 1960s, the movement would put into place some of its more famous strategies of peaceful resistance. The decade would witness "sit-ins" protesting desegregation at lunch counters, as well as the "freedom rides" where blacks and whites would oppose segregation on interstate travel by traveling on integrated busses. It was also during those early years of the decade where American people saw some of the most brutal pushback from some white southerners.

By 1963, King decided to concentrate his efforts on combating segregation and unequal treatment of African Americans in one of the most divisive places in the whole South: Birmingham, Alabama. It was the first time that MLK had personally and officially led a movement, and, as anticipated, the hot-headed segregationist and Birmingham public safety commissioner "Bull" Connor sent out dogs and police with clubs and high-powered water hoses at the peaceful protesters. The entire event was shown on national television to a shocked public. And although not much changed in Alabama, King and his SCLC made their point. They showed the world what life was like for a black person living in the South. It was also following these events that President JFK sent to Congress a bill that would, after his death, become the Civil Rights Act of 1964.

Following the march in Birmingham, which proved a winning tactic for King and his movement, MLK led his greatest march on Washington, D.C. Thousands would hear him give his most famous speech from the stairs of the Lincoln Memorial. For the first time, the non-violent movement was being listened to. Then, just weeks after the historic "I Have a Dream Speech," a bomb exploded at the 16th Street Baptist Church in Birmingham, killing four young girls. And just two months after that, an assassin's bullet found President Kennedy. His successor, Lyndon B. Johnson, used the events in Alabama as motivation to do anything in his power to push Kennedy's Civil Rights bill through Congress. And he did just that. On July 2, 1964, the president

Prior to the death of Jimmie Lee Jackson and the subsequent Selma march, it was the Civil Rights Act of 1964 that garnered all the media attention pertaining to civil rights. The Reverend Martin Luther King, Jr., is seen speaking about the passage of the act during the Senate debate in 1964 (photograph by Marion S. Trikosko, Library of Congress).

signed the Civil Rights Act of 1964, prohibiting discrimination because of race, religion, national origin, or gender.[6] After nearly 100 years, segregation was finally over.

Yet, one significant change remained elusive. One without which there really would never be any lasting change—the right of all African Americans to vote. The year 1964 kicked off what became known as "Freedom Summer," where young SNCC workers, joined by a new group called the Congress of Racial Equality (CORE), began a campaign to register as many African Americans as they could to vote in the South. Focusing mainly on Mississippi, where the discrepancy in those eligible to vote and registered to do so was the highest in the nation, the groups hoped to draw enough media attention to hopefully encourage Congress to act and pass a comprehensive voting rights act.

The campaign was off to a rough start, yet still managed to register many people. SNCC and CORE recruited many white male and female college students to go to Mississippi and help with the voter registration to strengthen the movement. Many hoped that this would receive some national publicity and deter much violence as this time it would be directed equally against whites and blacks. Yet, the racial beatings, intimidation, and, in some cases, even murder continued. In June 1964, three young men, two of whom were white, were stopped by a local Klansman and police officer for a bogus traffic violation. They would never come home that night. Their bodies would later be discovered after an extensive search initiated by a shocked LBJ and an angry American public now starting to pay attention to what was happening in the Deep South.

Yet, almost two years into the voting rights campaign, the violent pushback from local law enforcement and the indifference coming from Capitol Hill and the president severely hindered any major success. As far as the federal government was concerned, their job was finished when Congress passed the Civil Rights Act of 1964.

By 1965, Selma, Alabama, became the most glaring problem for the SCLC, SNCC, and CORE. In the year prior, more than 2,000 African Americans had been arrested in demonstrations, yet little had changed regarding the black vote.[7] About half of Selma's population was African American. And regardless of the new Civil Rights Act, segregation was still rampant on buses and in schools, parks, restaurants, and public swimming pools. As the white neighborhoods were dotted with beautiful single-family homes separated by perfectly paved roads, the black neighborhoods were riddled with old multi-family buildings and dirt roads. With income discrepancy at an all-time high with relation to the rest of the nation, Selma needed new leadership. The issue was that the voting campaign in the city and numerous demonstrations up to this point had led to only 23 black voting registrations. By the time Jimmie Lee Jackson stepped out of the Baptist church on that night of February 18, 1965, to protest the arrest of a civil rights activist taken into custody, Martin Luther King Jr.'s attention was already turned towards Selma. Yet it would be Jimmie's death that would make Selma MLK's newest frontline battlefield in his war against the segregationist clutches of the ole South.

* * * * * *

Dr. King visited Jimmie Lee Jackson at the Good Samaritan Hospital in Selma a few days after the shooting. Lee would live four more days before he succumbed to his injuries. Speaking at his eulogy to the hundreds of people who packed the Zion Methodist Church, MLK would recall, "I never will forget as I stood by his bedside a few days ago ... how radiantly he still responded, how he mentioned the freedom movement and how he talked about the faith that he still had in his God. Like every self-respecting Negro, Jimmie Jackson wanted to be free.... We must be concerned not merely about who murdered him but about the system, the way of life, the philosophy which produced the murder."[8] King had been present in Selma without much success since January 1965, a full month before the fatal shooting. Up to that point, the hope that Sheriff Jim Clark would be unable to keep his hatred towards the idea of desegregation in check did not come to fruition. Along with it, King did not get the media presence he desired, nor the potential pull in evoking major legislative change that came with it. All of that, however, was about to change.

Dr. King proclaimed in a *New York Times* article that "Selma has succeeded in limiting Negro legislation to the snail's pace of about 145 persons a year. At this rate, it would take 103 years to register the 15,000 eligible Negro voters of Dallas County."[9] The area was also exploitable due to Selma's Sheriff Clark, who was known to be brutal in suppressing demonstrations. As unfortunate as violence towards peaceful protesters was, there was also no doubt about how much publicizing it could work towards revitalizing the civil rights movement, which many believed had ended with the passage of the 1964 legislation.

Quickly exploiting the sheriff's violence, just days before Jackson's shooting in February, MLK led potential voters to the Selma courthouse to register them to vote. And although the federal judge's ruling supported the action, Clark and the city of Selma did not. Police pounced on the marchers and even beat a few. King publicly admitted that he wanted to get arrested to make it known what Selma was doing to blacks attempting to register to vote. Following 770 arrests—which included MLK and many school children—on the first day of the march, the sheriff followed suit by imprisoning another 820 African Americans for parading without a permit in the days that followed. Yet, "as Clark became more high-handed and brutal," stated historian Harvard Sitkoff, "he contained himself enough to frustrate King's SCLC's calculated strategy of confrontation."[10] The events failed to bring out any national indignation. At least enough to move the needle on any federal action.

After news of Jackson's death became known in the community, SCLC organizer James Bevel stated bluntly, "We will march Jimmie's body to the state capitol in Montgomery and lie [sic] it on the steps so Governor George Wallace can see what he's done."[11] To King, Bevel hit the nail on the head. As the Southern Christian Leadership Council prepared their march from Selma to Montgomery—sans the body—they put out a pamphlet stating it was Jackson's death that served as "the catalyst that produced the march."[12] The trudge began on a Sunday, March 7, at the Edmund Pettus Bridge; it had been four days since Jackson's funeral. It would be a 50-mile march, but the approximately 600 men, women, and children—including 80 Alabama whites—would not be deterred. As TV cameras rolled and numerous journalists scribbled notes in their notepads, the hundreds of freedom-loving and singing activists set off for the state's capital. As they were about to cross the bridge, they were met by hundreds of state troopers commanded by Major John Cloud, barring the other end. "You have two minutes to turn around and go back to your church." He did not wait for a response: "Troopers forward!"

What came to be known in American history books as "Bloody Sunday" would turn the bullet that entered Jimmie Lee Jackson's body on the night of February 18, 1965, into a catalyst for one of the most monumental pieces of legislation to ever come out of Congress. Millions watched from home as their TV sets showed state troopers attacking peaceful marchers with clubs and tear gas. They were aghast. How could this still be happening in the United States? Was this really what southern states were willing to do in order to prevent blacks from attaining the equal right to vote? Unfortunately for the nation at the time, the answer to both of those questions was a resounding yes. Writing about the events years later, Sitkoff described how besieged with demands for federal intervention the White House had become in just those first 24 hours: "Some four hundred rabbis, pastors, and nuns rushed to Selma, and at least ten times that number of clergymen converged on Washington to press Congress for voting-rights legislation and to denounce the President for his 'unbelievable lack of action' in the crisis."[13] Thousands of blacks and whites would lead their own sympathy marches across the nation to showcase unity. Yet, fearing more violence, all President Johnson could do was to ask King to call off the renewed effort to march once more. Dr. King would not comply.

The civil rights march from Selma to Montgomery, Alabama, 1965, showed unity among the races as well as religions (photograph by Peter Pettus, Library of Congress).

As thousands more people from across the nation arrived to join the cause, Johnson could no longer stand idle. With the world watching, this time under the guidance and protection of federalized National Guard troops ordered by the president, the peaceful marchers finally completed their task. Four days after they set off on a 12-hour-a-day march, the marchers reached Montgomery on March 25, 1965. A week prior, a horrified LBJ went on national television and called on Congress to pass a new voting rights bill. "There is no Negro problem. There is no Southern problem. There is no Northern problem. There is only an American problem," said the president. "Their cause must be our cause too. Because it is not just Negros, but really it is all of us who must overcome the crippling legacy of bigotry and injustice. And we shall overcome."[14]

* * * * *

The Selma to Montgomery march became the pinnacle of the movement, at the time it was already splintering into factions. It became once more, albeit temporarily, united together under the leadership of Martin Luther King. Historian Stephen Oates described Selma as "the [Civil Rights] Movement's finest hour," and King himself would say that the national criticism of "Bloody Sunday" was "a shining moment in the conscience of man."[15]

It was no secret that by 1965, the leading civil rights groups—the SNCC, SCLC, CORE, and NAACP—and the followers of Elijah Muhammad and his most famous disciple Malcolm X had begun to drift in opposite directions. The younger members turned against the more established organizations and MLK specifically. The prominent leader was suddenly seen as too slow and compromising when it came to pushing for change. Others turned their efforts to the North, where instead of segregation, African Americans faced oppressive racism. And still, others advocated against anti-violence as a means of fighting prejudice.

Specifically to those African Americans living in the bustling ghettos of northern metropolitan areas, it was becoming apparent that simply winning political rights for African Americans would not right the ills of economic inequality between the races. Poor living conditions, higher rates of illness and infant mortality, and juvenile delinquency and crime rates were all typical. And while the civil rights movement had raised their hopes for a better future, in 1965 African Americans could scarcely see any real hope for socio-economic advancement. Many found themselves pushed into low-paying jobs in factories. By mid-decade, only 15 percent of African Americas held professional, managerial, or clerical jobs, compared to 44 percent of whites. Similarly, the average income of African American families was 55 percent that of their white counterparts.[16]

The impatience with King's seemingly slow gains led to the radicalization of the movement the young reverend helped create. Calling for "Black Power," CORE and SNCC's new leaders, including Stokely Carmichael, called for banning any white membership within their organizations and a renewed focus on emphasizing black distinctiveness and culture instead of assimilation MLK had been calling for. This would be a movement to end racial oppression, take pride in one's culture, and gain economic self-sufficiency. It would also be more direct, militant, and based on self-defense—directly countering the preachings of MLK up to that point. The movement was fragmenting, showing the beginning of its end. In a sense, the Selma march stemming from the fatal

shooting of Jimmie Lee Jackson was the last time the civil rights movement fought as the embodiment of its once-true self, unbroken and
united for a common cause. The splintering of the civil rights movement
and its shift towards more direct and sometimes violent and militant
actions would have a negative effect on bringing more white supporters
to its cause. In fact, this new shift in public opinion that was now seeing the movement as inducing violence was making any potential future
legislation to help African Americans less likely by the day. The bullet
fired at Jackson and the subsequent push for one last major legislation
spurred on the last time that the movement, which would be declared
all but over after the assassination of MLK in just three years, managed
to get the federal government to enact monumental legislation.

Congress passed the Voting Rights Act of 1965 on August 6, 1965,
suspending all literacy tests and poll taxes, which hindered most blacks
from attaining the right to vote. The act also authorized the attorney
general to send federal examiners to register voters in any county with
less than fifty percent of the voting-age population registered.[17] The new
provisions were further bolstered by the final adaptation of the 1964's
Twenty-Fourth Amendment to the Constitution, which read: "The right
of citizens of the United States to vote in any primary or other election
... shall not be denied or abridged by the United States or any other State
by reason of failure to pay any poll tax or other tax."[18] Together, the Voting Rights Act of 1965 and the new amendment created the opportunity for many blacks to register to vote for the first time in their adult
lives. In 1960, only 20 percent of blacks of voting age had been registered to vote; by 1964, the figure had risen 39 percent, and by 1971 it was
62 percent.[19]

Lyndon Johnson never missed an opportunity to point out the historical implications of the passage of the Voting Rights Act. In fact, he
viewed it as one of his most significant accomplishments in office. When
cameras captured the president signing the legislation into law in the
presence of Dr. King and numerous other civil rights leaders, the room
chosen for the occasion was the same in which Lincoln had written the
Emancipation Proclamation nearly 100 years before. During the cere-
mony, LBJ recalled "the outrage of Selma" and referred to the right to
vote as "the most powerful instrument ever devised by man for breaking
down injustice and destroying the terrible walls which imprison men
because they are different from other men."[20] Speaking in his annual

address to the Southern Christian Leadership Council a few days after the famous signing, MLK noted that "Montgomery led to the Civil Rights Act of 1957 and 1960; Birmingham inspired the Civil Rights Act of 1964 and Selma produced the Voting Rights Legislation of 1965."[21]

Yet, apart from the Civil Rights Act of 1968, pushed through Congress in the wake of King's assassination and in his honor, the Voting Rights Act was truly the last bipartisan legislation. Violence and lack of direct and centralized authority and leadership led to actions that further alienated the white population against the movement. Barely a week after the passage of the historic voting law in 1965, a riot erupted in the Watts neighborhood of Los Angeles. The uprising would last nearly a week, spurred on by police brutality towards African Americans in the area. In the end, 14,000 National Guard members and 1,500 law officers were needed to restore order and stop the violence and looting. The rioters burned and looted entire neighborhoods and destroyed about $45 million in property, killing 34 people and injuring another 900.[22]

The Watts riots inspired similar actions in major cities across the nation for the next three years. In 1967, violent protests and property damage in Detroit resulted in nearly 50 deaths and prompted the U.S. government to send in tanks and soldiers to contain the fallout. About 4,000 fires destroyed 1,300 buildings, and the damage in property neared $250 million.[23] Public opinion towards the civil rights struggle had shifted from general openness towards disdain. Jimmie Jackson's inspiring death and the subsequent Selma march and passage of the Voting Rights Act of 1965 could not have happened at any other time in the 1960s. If delayed any more, the environment for real legislative change on a national level would have proved to be impossible to attain.

Jimmie Lee Jackson is remembered by those who knew him as an eager youth from Alabama who cared deeply for his mother. What about those who never did? According to a historian at the National Civil Rights Museum (NCRM), "the death of Jackson goes unremembered." The historian laments that this is perhaps ironic considering that "had it not been for the murder of Jimmie Lee, it is probable that 'Bloody Sunday' would not have occurred."[24] And if that were the case, what of the march from Selma to Montgomery? What of the Voting Rights Act of 1965? The irony of it further lies in the fact that Jackson seemed to have been on his way to recovery once in the hospital. While he was sitting up and in good spirits, doctors convinced him to have a second surgery, which even at the time seemed debatable. His doctors realized that his blood was turning darker during this procedure, and Jimmie needed to be put on 100 percent oxygen. But it was too late. Jimmie Lee Jackson stopped breathing and passed away on the operating table. Days later, and once more weeks after, thousands of people gathered in his honor to march on Alabama's state capital to demand change. And now, decades later, Ryan M. Jones of the NCRM asks the question that begs asking: "Fifty years later, who mourns for Jimmie Lee Jackson?"[25]

For Further Reading

Juan Williams's *Eyes on the Prize: America's Civil Rights Years, 1954–1965* (1987), which is technically a companion to the multi-part PBS television series, does a great job covering the Selma march and the events leading up to it in the topic's dedicated section of the book. Similarly, a lot of this chapter relied on Harvard Sitkoff's *The Struggle for Black Equality* (1981), which places in context King's need for a new Birmingham—Selma would fit the bill—to garner the attention of the media. While not about Selma, the autobiographies of both Martin Luther King and Malcolm X are must-reads when trying to understand the leadership, successes, and failures of the civil rights movement. Lastly, Steve Fiffer and Adar Cohen published one of the only accounts dedicated to the story of Jimmie Lee Jackson and the significance of his death to Selma, as well as the movement as a whole. Titled *Jimmie Lee & James: Two Lives, Two Deaths, and the Movement That Changed America* (2015), the book recounts the tragic events by interweaving them with those surrounding the death of James Reeb, a Boston minister who also died in the protests leading up to the Selma march. Full of details about the weeks and months surrounding the deaths of the two men, the book makes an argument similar to the one made in this chapter, namely that their deaths spurred on a stagnant movement.

13

Sins of Our Fathers, March 16, 1968

A U.S. congressman sat at his desk on Capitol Hill, staring at the letter in his hands. He placed it down on the desk in front of him and reached for a glass of water, his gaze never leaving the letter in front of him.

Gentlemen,

It was late in April 1968 that I first heard of "Pinkville" and what allegedly happened there. I received the first report with much skepticism. But in the following months, I was to hear similar stories from such a wide variety of people that it became impossible for me to disbelieve that something rather dark and bloody did occur sometime in March 1968 in a village called "Pinkville" in the Republic of Vietnam....

One village area was particularly troublesome and seemed to be infested with booby traps and enemy soldiers.... One morning ... Task Force Barker moved out from its firebase and headed for "Pinkville." Its mission: destroy the trouble spot and all of its inhabitants. When "Butch" told me this I didn't quite believe that what he was telling me was true, but he assured me that it was....

Any villagers who ran from Charlie Company were stopped by the encircling companies. I asked "Butch" several times if all the people were killed. He said that he thought they were—men, women, and children.

He recalled seeing a small boy, about three or four years old, standing by the trail with a gunshot wound in one arm. The boy was clutching his wounded arm with his other hand, while blood trickled between his fingers. He was staring around himself in shock and disbelief at what he saw. "He just stood there with big eyes staring around like he didn't understand; he didn't believe what was happening. Then the captain RTO (radio operator) put a burst of M16 fire into him." ...

Sincerely,
Ron Ridenhour[1]

He then did what most of his colleagues had done since the letters started arriving a few months back—ignored it. As for Ron Ridenhour, he did not yet know it, but his letter—which he had sent to countless congressmen and even President Nixon himself—would forever alter how Americans would view the Vietnam War. For now, however, justice for the nearly 400 innocent victims would have to wait.

* * * * * *

Public support for the Vietnam War was already waning when news of the Mỹ Lai massacre was revealed to the world in November 1969 with *Time* and *Life* magazine articles detailing the contents of Ridenhour's letter. As the floodgates opened, the massacre in two hamlets of Sơn Mỹ village in Quảng Ngãi Province, marked on U.S. topographic maps of Vietnam as Mỹ Lai and Mỹ Khê, became front-page news. (The term "Pinkville" used by Ron Ridenhour in his letter referred to the military maps used in the field, which showed congested areas in pink.) Coupled with the ongoing antiwar protest and following 1968, one of the most tumultuous years in American history, the news of American soldiers' atrocities would create in the nation a crisis of conscience unmatched in its long history. As stated by Kenneth C. Davis years later, "America was forced to look at itself in a manner once reserved for enemies who had committed war crimes."[2]

It would be an understatement to say that not everyone marched off to war proudly ready to sacrifice their lives for their country. The antiwar movement had begun almost as soon as the war began to escalate in 1964. Some opposed it on the basis that the United States had no business meddling in what amounted to a civil war in Vietnam. Others questioned the validity of the supposed "good" side of South Vietnam, which under the leadership of Ngô Đình Diệm seemed no better than a dictatorship. And still others saw it as a waste of funds and effort that could be better utilized back home in fighting the Cold War against the Soviet Union. Some people—a small percentage—opposed the war in Vietnam on the grounds of morality. But that was about to change.

The antiwar movement coincided with the growth of student activism and the organization of what became known in history as the New Left movement, with the "new" referring to a departure from the "old" liberalism of the 1930s New Deal policies and a move towards a more socialist society. As the war in Vietnam began to escalate, students across the nation's campuses found an issue behind which they could all assemble in protest. By April 1965, the Students for a Democratic

Society—an organization calling for participatory democracy and more individual freedom—helped organize a march on Washington, D.C., by some 20,000 protesters. By November, a similar protest rally drew another 30,000 people.[3] Soon the antiwar movement expanded past just college-age students and added returning veterans who spoke of the war's atrocities. In the spring of 1967, nearly half a million people gathered in New York City's Central Park, shouting, "Burn [draft] cards, not people!" and "Hell no, we won't go!" One protester explained:, "We were having no effect on U.S. policy, so we thought we had to up the ante."[4] It was obvious that Vietnam was beginning to draw lines and divide America.

Still, despite the ever-growing antiwar movement, a poll taken in December 1967 showed that 70 percent of Americans backed the U.S. involvement in the war and believed that the antiwar protests were "acts of disloyalty."[5] But then things went from bad to worse in 1968, when the Tet Offensive showed the American people that, contrary to what they heard from their leadership, the United States was not winning this war.

January 30, 1968, was the Vietnamese equivalent of New Year's Eve, known in Vietnam as Tet. Taking advantage of a temporary truce, the Communist Vietcong launched an unprecedented and overwhelming attack on more than 100 towns and cities across South Vietnam, catching the U.S. forces entirely by surprise. And although American forces were able to repel the attack, the psychological damage was done. The American public, which had been repeatedly told that the war in Vietnam was being won, was shocked. A news survey showed that directly after the Tet Offensive, the nation was now evenly divided among those favoring and opposing the war—a significant change in just a few months since the last poll was taken.[6] And while the events would spell the beginning of the end of the presidency of Lyndon Johnson, his successor would not do much better.

During the first few months of his presidency, Richard Nixon faced a jaded and distraught public. Although he promised an end to the war in 1968, it would drag out to arguably 1973 and cost an additional 20,000 American lives. Even after the gradual pullout of American armed forces began in 1969, the events from the war continued to divide the public. And then, on November 12, 1969, a *New York Times* investigative journalist broke the Mỹ Lai story to the Associated Press.

Bullets That Changed America

Within a week, it was being carried by all the major weekly news outlets. Soon, members of the Congress, in some instances the very same ones who had ignored the letters Ron Ridenhour had sent, as well as all major news outlets, who up to this point would also not touch the story, suddenly expressed horror and began calling for an investigation. The American soldiers, the majority of whom had nothing to do with the massacre and were drafted into the war against their will, received the moniker "baby killers." The reputation of Vietnam War veterans was tarnished forever. What was perhaps just as damning for the American public was that these events had taken place months prior. They had been covered up by their government and without repercussions to those responsible.

* * * * * *

It was 7:22 a.m. on March 16 when nine helicopters carrying Charlie Company lifted off from a U.S. base in the jungles of Vietnam. Their destination, Mỹ Lai 4. Traveling above what seemed like an endless wilderness, the choppers passed by other helicopters coming back from securing a simple small rice paddy for their arrival. The helicopters touched down, nearly 150 meters west of Mỹ Lai's houses, with the door gunners opening up with suppressive fire into the vacant field around them. "Move with extreme caution and return any fire," ordered one of the officers.[7] After marking the landing zone with additional smoke bombs to show their location for any reinforcements that might be needed, the men began to move in on the village. The commanding officer of Charlie Company, Ernest Medina, and his command group moved within reach of the 40 or so irregularly spaced huts separated by trees and foliage and set up their command post. The officer then ordered one platoon to stay back just outside the town and west of the landing zone, as he sent two forward for inspection. Medina's third platoon took on more of a supportive and inactive role in what was about to transpire ahead of him.

The first and second platoons of Lieutenant Calley and Lieutenant Stephen Brooks swept down into the Mỹ Lai village, home to approximately 700 inhabitants. It was 8:00 a.m. As the men walked among the sheds and tiny homes, they encountered families, women, and children, mostly cooking rice for breakfast outside their homes. The process that followed was standard for a "search and destroy" mission. The soldiers dragged men and women outside of their homes and interrogated them at gunpoint, all the while searching for the previously reported Vietcong enemy guerrilla forces among them. Fed up and aggravated with not finding what they were looking for, one man, off to the side from the main group, stabbed an old man in the back with his bayonet as the elder turned his back towards him to go back in the house.

Calley ordered the men to round up occupants into groups and direct them into the center of the hamlet. For many of the soldiers, memories of traps and sniper fire that had killed 100 of Charlie Company's men in just the past couple of months were still very vivid.

A group of around 15 women and children were gathered off to the side of the main huddle. "No VC [Vietcong]! No VC!" they called to Calley. Standing near them with his M16 rifle pointed at the group was a young soldier, Paul Meadlo. "You know what I want you to do with them," said the commanding officer angrily. As Calley walked away, Meadlo stood there shaking. He was still there when the officer returned a few minutes later, the rifle still in his hands, finger still on the trigger. "Haven't you got rid of them yet? I want them dead. Waste them!"[8] The baby-faced 22-year-old Paul looked at the face of a woman in front of him. She stopped crying. The young man closed his eyes and pulled the trigger.

Calley next to him followed with its own burst of fire a second after. "I poured about four clips into the group ... the mothers were hugging their children.... Well, we kept right on firing," recalled Meadlo.[9] Other witnesses would later remember tears falling down Meadlo's face.[10] "That day in Mỹ Lai, I was personally responsible for killing about twenty-five people. Personally. Men, women," recalled Varnado Simpson, a member of Lieutenant Calley's unit. "From shooting them, to cutting their throats, scalping them, to cutting off their hands and cutting out their tongues. I did it. I just went. My mind just went."[11] When later asked what his directive had been, another soldier answered, "Kill anything that breathed."[12]

It was around 10:00 a.m. when Medina's Third Platoon set off towards the village. Of his entry into Mỹ Lai from the south, Captain Medina later recalled: "I saw some bodies at a distance ... [but] I did not go over and check them out."[13] The 30 or so bodies seen on the outskirts of the village belonged to women and children. But Medina and his men would not have known that. In fact, it was later revealed that they were most likely unaware of the details of what had transpired inside the village, and all things considered, believed the firefight they were hearing was with the Vietcong. From there, the captain and his command group moved through Mỹ Lai's burning houses and blown-up bunkers. Made more difficult by the smoke, the backup team did not at first realize what they were all looking at as they descended deeper into the village proper. Among the incoming group was army photographer Ronald Haeberle. He would later recall realizing for the first time that bodies of innocent civilians were scattered around them, more than he could count at the moment—killed by American soldiers at point-blank range. At one point, the photographer focused his lens on a young toddler just a few feet away, but before he could press the shutter button, the boy was torn apart by rifle fire.[14] The shooting was not yet over.

On the other side of the small village, the carnage continued. Having herded nearly 80 more civilians to a nearby drainage ditch, Calley ordered his men to push whole families with women and children into the pit and open fire. While some soldiers, visibly shaken and crying, refused the order, others gladly obeyed. When a small child, not older than three, began running away, Calley captured him, threw him on top of the freshly killed bodies in the ditch, and promptly executed him. Around this time, Chief Warrant Officer Hugh Thompson found himself piloting his helicopter directly above the ditch. While visibility was still poor, he later recalled that something did not feel right to him, prompting him to take a closer look. On his downward approach, the officer could make out the GIs shooting into the large hole in the ground. And then he saw a child being dragged in and thrown into the ditch. Placing his helicopter between the soldiers and a group of young children being forcibly taken towards the ditch, Thompson ordered his helicopter crew to shoot anyone who tried to stop him. With machine guns drawn towards members of Charlie Company, the helicopter pilot scooped up the few children into his helicopter and took off. His was the last good deed of the otherwise tragic day.

"Kill civilians? I've killed civilians myself—because I was ordered to," admitted a soldier months after the fact. "But I only found out afterward that they were civilians." To soldiers such as himself, this was a complicated situation without much moral repercussion. A logical choice of sorts. "At the time, how do you know? Because it's a woman? No, because women can fire AK47s. Because they are children? No, because they can make boobytraps."[15] Following a similar train of thought, Paul Meadlo, trying to explain his role in the killings, stated: "At the time I felt like I was doing the right thing because, like I said, I lost buddies ... lost a damn good buddy."[16] Another Vietnam veteran, having spent nearly three years in the jungles of Indochina, tried to comprehend why such an event would ever be possible. And while admitting that was not forgivable, he tried to place it in context: "For one thing, the same sense of frustration and doubt and seeming illogic about the war that divides the nation in some ways also divides the troops fighting [it]." He added: "There are no battle lines in the war. So many tens of thousands of civilians have been killed and wounded, so many hundreds of thousands made refugees, that their fate registers with less shock." According to the soldier, this was further compounded by the fact that "un-uniformed guerrilla 'civilians,' including women and children Viet Cong, have caused enough U.S. casualties that respect for civilian status diminishes."[17]

Yet, no matter how the event was explained, by 11:00 a.m. on March 16, 1968, the words "Mỹ Lai" would transition from being a mere name of a physical place into a symbol of an event that many to this day still cannot shake or ignore. Officially, the operation was reported back to army headquarters as a resounding success—around 130 enemies dead and only one American wounded. Ironically, it would later come out that the lone casualty was a soldier who had shot himself in the foot to avoid having to carry out the execution orders. After Thompson filed a report alleging war crimes, the army conducted a brief investigation. They interviewed those involved and concluded that only about twenty-odd civilians had died as collateral damage. Case closed. Nearly two years later, army investigators, having reopened the case after the publishing of Ronald Ridenhour's letter, discovered three mass graves in Mỹ Lai. They contained the bodies of about 500 villagers.[18]

* * * * * *

Ridenhour's letter would go ignored by President Nixon, members of the Pentagon, the State Department, Joint Chiefs of Staff, and numerous members of Congress.[19] That is until its contents showed up on the front pages of all major news publications worldwide well over a year after the event in 1969. After General Westmoreland ordered an investigation and countless witnesses were finally interviewed on the record, the lid was officially blown off of any denial of the atrocities perpetrated by the U.S. armed forces. By the time the investigation was concluded in late 1970, it was followed by a plethora of court-martials for dereliction of duty—mainly stemming from the event's cover-up. And although many individuals would go on to be demoted, and some even found guilty of murder in further trials in 1971, it was the nation and its people who were changed forever.

It would be impossible to pinpoint Paul Meadlo as the first to fire a fatal bullet on that day. Yet, symbolically, and perhaps even literally, witness testimonies corroborated that the main shooting of the civilians began after Lieutenant Calley ordered the young man to discharge his weapon and himself quickly followed suit. In the end, the investigation led to a reduction in rank for all of those involved. Four officers—Calley, Medina, Captain Eugene Kotouc, and Lieutenant Thomas Willingham—were promptly court-martialed, although three of them would later be acquitted.[20] Calley, who was found guilty of the premeditated murder of civilians, was initially sentenced to life in prison only for the sentence to be reduced to house arrest by President Nixon.

According to historian Robert Leckie in his all-encompassing study, *The Wars of America*, "My Lai became 'a kind of oriflamme for the antiwar movement.'" The event shook the nation and made it question its own humanity. "To realize that their own soldiers were no better than the Communists in their treatment of their allies was so wounding to American self-esteem that most of the people refused to believe it or else turned away from the war in disgust." Similarly, the historian would go on to contend that "the infuriating fact that the truth about the massacre had been suppressed by the Pentagon for 18 months, hung like a millstone around the neck of Richard Nixon as he became the fourth American President to pursue the policy of 'containment' in Vietnam."[21]

A *Time* piece from the time of Calley's conviction perhaps best described what many people were feeling: "Our boys in Vietnam have spoiled for me the feeling I've always had that Americans are nicer than other people—the good guys, who are in the right and win wars."[22] The same article would go on to say that the "crisis of conscience caused by the [Mỹ Lai] affair is a graver phenomenon than the horror following the assassination of President Kennedy ... historically, it is more crucial." In the simplest terms, there were no more neutral people left in the United States when it came to the Vietnam War.

---

13. Sins of Our Fathers, March 16, 1968

At a protest held in New York directly after Calley's court ruling, the future Secretary of State John Kerry read a statement for which he would be recognized for decades to come: "We only want this county to realize that it cannot try a Calley for something which generals and Presidents and our way of life encouraged him to do. And if you try him ... you must in fact try this country."[23] There is no question that the Mỹ Lai incident changed the course of the war back home. Jan Barry, a founder of the Vietnam Veterans Against the War, viewed Mỹ Lai as a symbol of the dilemma of his generation as well as an epitome of sorts for the entire conflict and the deep-rooted divisions it caused: "To kill on military orders and be a criminal, or to refuse to kill and be a criminal is the moral agony of America's Vietnam War generation. It is what has forced upward of sixty thousand young Americans, draft resisters and deserters to Canada, and created one hundred thousand military deserters a year."[24] Kerry simply verbalized what many were now thinking. Mỹ Lai mattered.

Days after the verdict in the Mỹ Lai case was announced in 1971, a Harris Poll reported that, for the first time in the conflict's history, the majority of Americans opposed the war. As for the military, the crisis in morality that ensued only further sped up the eventual withdrawal from the conflict. Coupled with the negative perception of the armed forces that met all returning soldiers, the war no longer seemed defensible, even for the most ardent patriots. Desertion rates, as well as absences-without-leave (AWOL), skyrocketed. The army desertion rate, which in 1966 had been 14.9 men per thousand, quadrupled to 73.5 in 1971, three times higher than the worst desertion rates of the Korean War.[25] The AWOL rates were just as high. In 1966 there were 57.2 AWOL incidents per thousand in the army; after the Mỹ Lai court cases of 1971, that number jumped to 176.9.[26] And just as the media perpetuated the perception of soldiers as killing machines during the uncovering and the subsequent trial of the Mỹ Lai troops, violence erupted on college campuses when soldiers fired into protesters at Kent State on May 4, 1970. Ten days later, similar violence rocked the mostly black college of Jackson State in Mississippi, where National Guardsmen confronted a group of antiwar demonstrators and discharged their rifles, killing two students and wounding 12 others.[27]

Unlike his World War II counterpart, the Vietnam veteran would not receive a hero's welcome. In fact, events such as the Mỹ Lai massacre

The cry to end the war in Vietnam was already heard and seen across national TV screens in 1967, a year before the events of the Mỹ Lai massacre. Picture taken in Washington, D.C., at the National Mobilization to End the War (photograph by Warren K. Leffler, Library of Congress).

and the subsequent shootings on college campuses saw to it that his legacy would be tarnished for decades to come. In the end, Vietnam became a losing war, something that Americans just could not accept. A war that made them rethink the good-versus-evil narrative. A war in which their soldiers had failed, not just physically and militarily speaking, but morally as good people. Thousands of young men were uprooted from small towns across the country, sent to hostile jungles with the most inhospitable conditions, and asked to risk their lives. Many, having witnessed their dearest friends do just that, came back to a place that no longer felt like home. They got neither "thank you for your service" cards nor invitations to speak at school assemblies. People read the news, and to many American citizens, the returning soldiers were nothing short of "baby killers."

FOR FURTHER READING

There are countless books written about the Vietnam War as a whole. They range from multi-volume collections detailing the entire narrative of the war to more personal firsthand accounts and memoirs. For a comprehensive and balanced account of the war, one need not look any further than Stanley Karnow's Pulitzer Prize winning *Vietnam: A History* (1983). Although it is nearly 900 pages long—depending on the edition—it provides a very linear and easy-to-understand narrative of the entire conflict incorporating all aspects, military, foreign, and domestic. For a specific account of the Mỹ Lai massacre, the best recommendation would be Michael Bilton's *Four Hours in My Lai* (1992). It is by far the most comprehensive and detailed account of the event, right down to each hour or sometimes even each minute. For those who prefer primary firsthand accounts, *My Lai: A Brief History with Documents* (1998) does a great job with its selections, which include many testimonies from the event and the court cases that followed.

Epilogue

It was not until I was deep into the research of these events that it dawned on me—and perhaps it should have done so much earlier considering the title of this book—that each of the monumental incidents described here began with someone's death. That is not entirely a new concept in our nation's history. After all, had it not been for the death of many known figures in the annals of America, the course of events we read about in our school textbooks would most definitely have been altered. Take the assassination of President William McKinley on September 6, 1901, as an example. He was but the third president to have been assassinated by a bullet and by no means of the same pedigree as Abraham Lincoln. This might make the event little more than a simple historical footnote or an answer to a trivia question asking for a list of the presidents assassinated in office. Yet, as shown through the stories you just read, the effects of the single bullet being fired often alter a given paradigm.

Had it not been for a young anarchist, Leon Czolgosz, firing a bullet into the president at the Pan-American Exposition in Buffalo, New York, we would perhaps not have a president whose face now graces Mount Rushmore. Teddy Roosevelt, who is often considered to be one of the greatest presidents in American history, was relegated to the office of the vice presidency by his political opponents as to make him insignificant. In fact, both Republicans and Democrats saw the appointment as a way to tame the young New Yorker from ever gaining any real foothold in the political arena or having any real power in American politics. All it took to alter that plan and the nation's fate was one bullet fired by a man who would otherwise never be known to history. Teddy Roosevelt, unlike his predecessor, would go on to define an era both at home and abroad. His progressive domestic policies would forever alter the relationship between government and businesses and employers and their employees. On the international front, the U.S. would take a more asser-tive role in the Western Hemisphere with Roosevelt's Corollary to the Monroe Doctrine—and with mixed results when discussing U.S. and Latin America relations for the remainder of the twentieth century.

The same could be said of the final bullet that killed President John F. Kennedy. Many historians and conspiracy theorists believe that the U.S. involvement in Vietnam would have taken a different course had Lyndon B. Johnson not become president when he did. Or even the fact that had it not been for the assassination of Martin Luther King, Jr., the splintering civil rights movement could have held on for longer. In the end, history is full of what-ifs. Some are bigger than others. Most are only known by the popularity of the greater-than-life figures who take center stage in their respective narratives. Yet, as seen through the sto-ries within these pages, it is more than possible for history to change because of one thing or one person. In our nation, as in any nation around the world, change begins with people. Individuals who make transcendent decisions that on the surface may appear only relevant to their own lives and to the situation they find themselves in. But his-tory does not work that way. As a high school history teacher for nearly two decades, I find it essential to show my students that their decisions, no matter how small, sometimes have consequences way beyond their intended purposes. Or, as is the case in the stories mentioned here, sometimes the decision to pull a trigger—whether lawfully or not—may have repercussions way beyond one's personal life.

Unfortunately, there might be something to the saying "violence is as American as cherry pie." If that is indeed the case—and putting on the news each night might just reaffirm it so—are we on the verge of another history-altering event? Despite the year 2020, in which I write this book, not having any large-scale school shootings on par with Col-umbine, the number of homicides increased by 36 percent. Similarly, the number of mass shootings, which are classified as incidents where four or more people are shot or killed, rose drastically to 600, an almost 50 percent increase over the 2019 count.[1] In Chicago alone, there were 3,237 shooting incidents in 2020, while in New York, that number was 1,824—in both instances more than a 50 percent increase.[2] Perhaps not ironically, a *Time* magazine article from late December 2020 stated that the year was also record-breaking regarding firearm purchases across the nation. But what does all of this mean? Placing the argument of gun

Epilogue

violence or the Second Amendment aside, if this book proves anything, it is that as the American people, we may be all but one bullet away from a history-altering event. One shot. That sure gives one something to think about.

Chapter Notes

Chapter 1

1. John Ferling, *A Leap in the Dark: The Struggle to Create the American Republic*, Oxford University Press, New York, 2003, 7.

2. "Washington and the French and Indian War," Mount Vernon, https://www.mountvernon.org/george-washington/french-indian-war/washington-and-the-french-indian-war/#_ftnref34, accessed December 11, 2020.

3. David Preston, "When George Washington Started a War," *Smithsonian*, https://www.smithsonianmag.com/history/when-young-george-washington-started-war-180973076/, accessed December 11, 2020.

4. George Washington, "Expedition to the Ohio, 1754," National Archives, https://founders.archives.gov/documents/Washington/01-01-02-0004-0002, accessed December 11, 2020.

5. *Ibid.*

6. Preston, "When George Washington Started a War."

7. *Ibid.*

8. Fred Anderson, *Crucible of War: The Seven Years' War and the Fate of the Empire in British North America, 1754–1766*, Vintage Books, New York, 2001, 43.

9. Robert Leckie, *The Wars of America*, Harper Perennial, New York, 1993, 42.

10. *Ibid.*, 44.

11. Paul Johnson, *The Founding Father: George Washington*, Harper Perennial, New York, 2009, 31.

12. David Muzzey, *A History of Our Country*, Ginn and Company, Boston, 1943, 103–104.

13. *Ibid.*

14. *Ibid.*

15. *Ibid.*

Chapter 2

1. Ruth Reynolds, "131 Years Ago Andrew Jackson Slew Charles Dickinson in Duel Born of Gossip," *Daily News*, New York, May 30, 1937, 10C.

2. *Ibid.*, 12C.

3. Richard Hofstadter, *The American Political Tradition and the Men Who Made It*, Vintage Books, New York, 1989, 64–65.

4. Eric Foner, *Give Me Liberty! An American History*, W.W. Norton & Company, New York, 2009, 350.

5. Hofstadter, *The American Political Tradition*, 67.

6. Muzzey, *A History of Our Country*, 270.

7. *Ibid.*, 271–271.

8. Hofstadter, *The American Political Tradition*, 65.

9. Ruth Reynolds, "131 Years Ago Andrew Jackson Slew Charles Dickinson in Duel Born of Gossip," 10C.

10. *Ibid.*

11. *Ibid.*

12. *Ibid.*

13. *Ibid.*, 12C.

14. *Ibid.*

15. *Ibid.*

16. John Morgan, *Our Presidents: The Chief Executives, from George Washington to Lyndon B. Johnson*, The

Macmillan Company, New York, 1969, 60.

17. *Ibid.*
18. *Ibid.*
19. *Ibid.*, 64.
20. Muzzey, *A History of Our Country*, 284.
21. Hofstadter, *The American Political Tradition*, 72.
22. Foner, *Give Me Liberty! An American History*, 360.
23. *Ibid.*, 361.
24. Muzzey, *A History of Our Country*, 292.
25. Kenneth C. Davis, *Don't Know Much About History*, Perennial, New York, 2004, 169.
26. Eric Foner, *Give Me Liberty! An American History*, 365.

Chapter 3

1. John Sugden, *Tecumseh's Last Stand*, University of Oklahoma Press, Oklahoma, 1985, 143.
2. *Ibid.*
3. *Ibid.*
4. *Ibid.*
5. James Klotter, *History Mysteries*, University Press of Kentucky, Kentucky, 1989, 25.
6. Elliot West, "Tecumseh's Last Stand," History Net, https://www.historynet.com/tecumsehs-last-stand.htm, accessed December 16, 2020.
7. *Ibid.*
8. "Tecumseh's Plea to the Choctaws and the Chickasaws" from *American Indian Literature: An Anthology*, edited by Alan R. Velie, University of Oklahoma Press, Oklahoma, 1991, 148–51.
9. Elliot West, "Tecumseh's Last Stand."
10. Richard H. Dillon, *North American Indian Wars*, Facts on File, Inc., New York, 1983, 61.
11. *Ibid.*, 70.
12. Robert Leckie, *The Wars of America*, Harper & Row, Publishers, New York, 1981, 266.
13. Richard H. Dillon, *North American Indian Wars*, Facts on File, Inc., New York, 1983, 71.
14. Elliot West, "Tecumseh's Last Stand."
15. Donald L. Fixicio, "Native Nations Content with the Legacy of the War of 1812," National Parks Service, https://www.nps.gov/articles/the-legacy-of-the-war-of-1812-in-tribal-communities.htm, accessed December 17, 2020.
16. Sugden, *Tecumseh's Last Stand*, 214.
17. Muzzey, *A History of Our Country*, 306.

Chapter 4

1. *American History*, Houghton Mifflin Harcourt, Orlando, FL, 2018, 353.
2. *Ibid.*
3. Muzzey, *A History of Our Country*, 366.
4. David M. Potter, *The Impending Crisis: American Before the Civil War, 1848–1861*, Harper Perennial, New York, 2011, 211.
5. "Statement of James Townsley, 1879," Kansas History, https://olatheschools.libguides.com/JohnBrown/PottawatomieKillings, accessed December 21, 2020.
6. *Ibid.*
7. *Ibid.*
8. *Ibid.*
9. *Ibid.*
10. Potter, *The Impending Crisis: American Before the Civil War, 1848–1861*, 213.
11. Davis, *Don't Know Much About History*, 214.
12. "Incident at Harpers Ferry," *Richmond Enquirer*, October 25, 1859.
13. Muzzey, *A History of Our Country*, 377.
14. *Ibid.*
15. J.G. Nicolay and John Hay, eds., *Complete Works of Abraham Lincoln*, New York, The Century Co., 1894, vol. 5, 314.
16. From a speech delivered before the United States Senate by Henry Clay,

February 1839, from *The American Civil War: When Will a Nation Divide Against Itself*, Scholastic Book Services, New York, 1968, 15.

17. *American History*, Houghton Mifflin Harcourt, Orlando, FL, 2018, 362.

Chapter 5

1. Kristopher D. White and Chris Mackowski, "How in the World Did They Shoot Stonewall Jackson?," History Net, https://www.historynet.com/how-in-the-world-did-they-shoot-stonewall-jackson.htm, accessed December 28, 2020.

2. *Ibid.*

3. *Ibid.*

4. "Who Shot Stonewall Jackson," *The Free Lance-Star*, https://fredericksburg.com/town_and_countycivil_war/who-shot-stonewall-jackson/article_d4da4d59-5fd0-5bfe-9d24-e4505662d08f.html, accessed December 28, 2020.

5. White and Mackowski, "How in the World Did They Shoot Stonewall Jackson?"

6. Muzzey, *A History of Our Country*, 407.

7. *Ibid.*, 408.

8. Frank A. O'Reilly, "The True Battle for Fredericksburg," American Battlefield Trust, https://www.battlefields.org/learn/articles/true-battle-fredericksburg, accessed December 29, 2020.

9. Muzzey, *A History of Our Country*, 397.

10. "Stonewall Jackson," history.com, https://www.history.com/topics/american-civil-war/stonewall-jackson, accessed December 29, 2020.

11. *Ibid.*

12. *Ibid.*

13. "Stonewall Jackson," history.com, https://www.history.com/topics/american-civil-war/battle-of-chancellorsville, accessed December 31, 2020.

14. Captain Richard Eggleston Wilbourn, letter to Col. C.J. Faulkner, May 1863, https://www.virginiahistory.

org/collections-and-resources/virginia-history-explorer/general-orders-no-61/eyewitness-account, accessed December 31, 2020.

15. Marvin P. Rozear and Joseph C. Greenfield, Jr., "Let Us Cross Over the River": The Final Illness of Stonewall Jackson, *The Virginia Magazine of History and Biography*, January 1995, Vol. 103, No. 1, pp. 29–46.

16. "Why Stonewall Jackson's Death Became a Legend for the Ages," The National Interest, https://nationalinterest.org/blog/buzz/why-stonewall-jacksons-death-became-legend-ages-119401, accessed December 31, 2020.

17. *Ibid.*

18. Rev. J. William Jones, D.D., *Christ in the Camp: Or Religion in the Confederate Army*, The Martin & Hoyt Co. Atlanta, GA., 1904, 75.

19. Joe D. Haines, Jr., "America's Civil War: Stonewall Jackson's Last Days," History Net, https://www.historynet.com/stonewall-jacksons-death.htm, accessed January 1, 2021.

20. Rozear and Greenfield, Jr., "Let Us Cross Over the River": The Final Illness of Stonewall Jackson, 44.

21. *Ibid.*, 34.

22. Darrell Laurant, "Stonewall Jackson's Death Reverberated Through the State," *The News & Advance*, https://newsadvance.com/news/local/stonewall-jacksons-death-reverberated-through-state/article_31022026-baa6-11e2-a202-001a4bcf6878.html, accessed January 2, 2021.

23. *Ibid.*

24. Allan R. Millett and Peter Maslowski, *For the Common Defense: A Military History of the United States of America*, Free Press, New York, 1994, 213.

Chapter 6

1. Muzzey, *A History of Our Country*, 489.

2. Ray Allen Billington, *American*

History After 1865, Littlefield, Adams, & Co., Ames, IA, 1953, 57.

3. John A. Krout and Arnold S. Rice, *United States Since 1865*, Harper & Row Publishers, New York, 1977, 56.

4. *American History*, 517.

5. *Ibid.*

6. Billington, *American History After 1865*, 63.

7. Eric Foner, *Give Me Liberty! An American History*, 595.

8. David Greenberg, "Anarchy in the U.S.," *Slate*, https://slate.com/news-and-politics/2000/04/anarchy-in-the-u-s.html, accessed January 19, 2021.

9. "Wild Mob's Work," *The Chicago Tribune*, May 4, 1886, 1.

10. *Ibid.*

11. *Ibid.*

12. *Ibid.*

13. *Ibid.*

14. *Ibid.*

15. *Ibid.*

16. Foner, *Give Me Liberty! An American History*, 594.

17. Billington, *American History After 1865*, 64.

18. James L. Roark, *Understanding the American Promise: A History*, Bedford/St. Martin, Boston, 2014, 565.

19. Muzzey, *A History of Our Country*, 490.

20. Howard Zinn, *A People's History of the United States: 1492–Present*, Harper Perennial, New York, 1995, 266.

21. *Ibid.*

22. "Police Statue Falls in Blast," *The Pantagraph*, Bloomington, IL, October 7, 1969, 1.

Chapter 7

1. "Massacre at Wounded Knee, 1890," EyeWitness to History, http://www.eyewitnesstohistory.com/knee.htm, accessed January 25, 2021.

2. James A. Henretta, *America: A Concise History, Volume 2: Since 1865*, Bedford/St. Martin's, Boston, 2002, 471.

3. Davis, *Don't Know Much About History*, 260.

4. *American History*, Houghton Mifflin Harcourt, Orlando, FL, 2018, 457.

5. Henretta, *America: A Concise History, Volume 2: Since 1865*, 471.

6. *Ibid.*

7. "Documents Relating to the Wounded Knee Massacre," Digital History, https://www.digitalhistory.uh.edu/disp_textbook.cfm?smtID=3&psid=1101, accessed January 27, 2021

8. "Full Fifty Slain: Indian Treachery Once More Made Manifest," *The Nebraska State Journal*, Lincoln, NE, December 30, 1890, 1.

9. *Ibid.*

10. *Ibid.*

11. "Documents Relating to the Wounded Knee Massacre," Digital History, https://www.digitalhistory.uh.edu/disp_textbook.cfm?smtID=3&psid=1101, accessed January 27, 2021.

12. *Ibid.*

13. *Ibid.*

14. "Worse and Worse," *The Washburn Leader*, Washburn, North Dakota, January 3, 1891, 4.

15. Dee Brown, *Bury My Heart at Wounded Knee*, Henry Holt and Company, New York, 1991, 444.

16. "Documents Relating to the Wounded Knee Massacre," Digital History, https://www.digitalhistory.uh.edu/disp_textbook.cfm?smtID=3&psid=1101, accessed January 27, 2021.

17. Henretta, *America: A Concise History, Volume 2*, 474.

18. Foner, *Give Me Liberty! An American History*, 579.

19. Walter LaFeber, *The American Century: A History of the United States Since the 1890s*, M.E. Sharpe, Armonk, NY, 2008, 423.

20. *Ibid.*

21. *Ibid.*

22. *Ibid.*

Chapter 8

1. Greg Grandin, *Empire's Workshop: Latin America, the United States, and*

the Rise of New Imperialism, A Holt Paperback, New York, 2006, 3.

2. Walter LaFeber, *Inevitable Revolutions: The United States in Central America*, W.W. Norton, New York, 1993, 35.

3. Thomas A. Bailey, *A Diplomatic History of the American People*, Ninth Edition, Prentice Hall, NJ, 1974, 554.

4. David F. Long, *The Outward View: History of United States Foreign Relations*, Rand McNally & Company, Chicago, 1963, 234.

5. Jeff Guinn, *War on the Border: Villa, Pershing, the Texas Rangers, and an American Invasion*, Simon & Schuster, New York, 2021, 36–37.

6. John Milton Cooper Jr., *Pivotal Decades: The United States, 1900–1920*, W.W. Norton, New York, 1990, 225.

7. Thomas A. Bailey, *A Diplomatic History of the American People*, 555.

8. Lowell L. Blaisdell, "Henry Wilson and the Overthrow of Madero," *The Southwestern Social Science Quarterly*, September 1962, Vol. 43, No. 2, pp. 126–135.

9. *Ibid.*, 130.

10. Guinn, *War on the Border*, 36.

11. *Ibid.*

12. John S.D. Eisenhower, *Intervention! The United States and the Mexican Revolution*, 1913–1917, 24.

13. Guinn, *War on the Border*, 37.

14. Eisenhower, *Intervention!*, 28.

15. Blaisdell, "Henry Wilson and the Overthrow of Madero," 134.

16. Eisenhower, *Intervention!*, 28.

17. Blaisdell, "Henry Wilson and the Overthrow of Madero," 135.

18. Muzzey, *A History of Our Country*, 615.

19. Saladin Ambar, "Woodrow Wilson: Foreign Affairs," *UVA Miller Center*, https://millercenter.org/president/wilson/foreign-affairs, accessed September 13, 2021.

20. Cooper, *Pivotal Decades: The United States, 1900–1920*, 225.

21. *Ibid.*, 628–629.

22. *Ibid.*, 226

23. David F. Long, *The Outward View:*

History of United States Foreign Relations, 238.

24. Eric Foner, *The Story of American Freedom*, W.W. Norton, New York, NY, 1998, 686.

Chapter 9

1. "Yeggs Kill Guard—Steal $20,000," *Boston Post*, Boston, MA, April 16, 1920, 30.

2. *American History*, Houghton Mifflin Harcourt, Orlando, FL, 2018, 714.

3. Foner, *The Story of American Freedom*, 131.

4. Woodrow Wilson, "State of the Union Address December 7, 1915," America History, http://www.let.rug.nl/usa/presidents/woodrow-wilson/state-of-the-union-1915.php, accessed February 1, 2021.

5. "Palmer Raids," history.com, https://www.history.com/topics/red-scare/palmer-raids, accessed February 1, 2021.

6. Cooper, Jr., *Pivotal Decades: The United States, 1900- 1920*, 328.

7. *Ibid.*

8. *American History*, Houghton Mifflin Harcourt, Orlando, FL, 2018, 713.

9. Davis, *Don't Know Much About History*, 325.

10. Emily Owens, "The Not So Roaring 20s," *New York Times*, October 1, 2011, https://www.nytimes.com/2011/10/02/opinion/sunday/the-not-so-roaring-20s.html, accessed February 1, 2021.

11. "Conductor Saw Vanzetti on Car; Identified the Prisoner and Sacco as Men Who Boarded Trolley at West Bridgewater," *The Boston Globe*, Boston, MA, June 26, 1920, 4.

12. "The Case of Sacco and Vanzetti," Massachusetts.gov, https://www.mass.gov/info-details/sacco-vanzetti-investigation-and-arrest, accessed February 2, 2021.

13. James West Davidson, and Mark Hamilton Lytle, *After the Fact: The Art of Historical Detection*, Volume 2, Alfred A. Knopf, New York, NY, 1982, 265.

14. "Sacco and Vanzetti Were Executed 90 Years Ago. Their Deaths Made History," https://time.com/4895701/sacco-vanzetti-90th-anniversary/, accessed February 2, 2021.

15. Davidson and Lytle, *After the Fact: The Art of Historical Detection*, 264.

16. *Ibid.*, 265.

17. Foner, *Give Me Liberty! An American History*, 721.

18. *American History*, Houghton Mifflin Harcourt, Orlando, FL, 2018, 714.

19. LaFeber, *The American Century: A History of the United States Since the 1890s*, 125.

20. *Ibid.*, 132.

21. *Ibid.*, 133.

22. *Ibid.*

23. "Stock Market Crash of 1929," history.com, https://www.history.com/topics/great-depression/1929-stock-market-crash, accessed February 3, 2021.

Chapter 10

1. "Heroes: Battle of Washington," *TIME Magazine*, http://content.time.com/time/subscriber/article/0,33009,744107,00.html, accessed February 6, 2021.

2. *Ibid.*

3. *Ibid.*

4. *Ibid.*

5. James Morgan, *Our Presidents*, The Macmillan Company, New York, NY, 1971, 330.

6. *Ibid.*, 331.

7. D. Duane Cummins and William Gee White, *Contrasting Decades: The 1920's and 1930's*, Glencoe Publishing Co., Inc., New York, NY, 1972, 187.

8. Walter LaFeber, *The American Century: A History of the United States Since the 1890s*, 154.

9. *Ibid.*

10. "Felons and Reds Led B.E.F. Rioting, Hoover Informed: Communists Given Blame by Mitchell," *The Philadelphia Inquirer*, Philadelphia, PA, September 12, 1932, 1–4.

11. "Soldiers Ordered Out in Washington After Fatal Police-Bonus Army Fray," *Miami News Record*, Miami, OK, July 28, 1932, 1.

12. "Regulars Move Like Giant Machine, Tanks Lumber Into Camps, B.E.F. Put to Rout," *The News-Herald*, Franklin, PA, July 29, 1932, 6.

13. *Ibid.*

14. *Ibid.*

15. *Ibid.*

16. "Troops Destroy Last Bonus Camp Vestiges," *The Miami Herald*, Miami, FL, July 30, 1932, 4.

17. *Ibid.*

18. "Felons and Reds led B.E.F. Rioting, Hoover Informed: Communists Given Blame by Mitchell," *The Philadelphia Inquirer*, Philadelphia, PA, September 12, 1932, 4.

19. *Ibid.*

20. "Texas Congressman Deplores Use of Troops," *The Miami Herald*, Miami, FL, July 30, 1932, 4.

21. "Hoover Is Criticized for Calling Troops, *The Miami Herald*, Miami, FL, July 30, 1932, 4.

22. "Bonus Army Dispersal 'Callous Barbarism,'" *The Miami Herald*, Miami, FL, July 30, 1932, 4.

23. Thomas Craughwell, "Hoover's Attack on the Bonus Army (Top 10 Mistakes by U.S. Presidents)," Britannica, http://blogs.britannica.com/2009/01/6-hoovers-attack-on-the-bonus-army-top-10-mistakes-by-us-presidents/, accessed February 9, 2021.

24. "French Press Sarcastic in Comments on Riot," *The Miami Herald*, Miami, FL, July 30, 1932, 4.

25. "German Newspaper Sees 'Hoover's End,'" *The Miami Herald*, Miami, FL, July 30, 1932, 4.

26. "London Newspaper Has Moral for Riot," *The Miami Herald*, Miami, FL, July 30, 1932, 4.

27. *American History*, Houghton Mifflin Harcourt, Orlando, FL, 2018, 775.

28. David E. Hamilton, "Herbert Hoover: Campaigns and Elections," UVA Miller Center, https://millercenter.org/president/hoover/campaigns-and-elections, accessed February 9, 2021.

29. Henretta, *America: A Concise History, Volume 2: Since 1865*, 715–716.

30. *Ibid.*

Chapter 11

1. "Five Slain at Station," *Kansas City Star*, Kansas City, MO, June 17, 1933, 1.

2. "Notorious Southwest Bandit Gang Falls Before Driving Force of Federal Agents," *The Reading Times*, Reading, PA, October 10, 1933, 10.

3. David Grann, *Killers of the Flower Moon: The Osage Murders and the Birth of the FBI*, Vintage, New York, NY, 2017, 116.

4. *Ibid.*, 113.

5. *Ibid.*

6. "The FBI and the American Gangster," FBI, https://www.fbi.gov/history/brief-history/the-fbi-and-the-american-gangster, accessed August 30, 2021.

7. Tim Weiner, *Enemies: A History of the FBI*, Random House, New York, NY, 2012, 63.

8. Curt Gentry, *J. Edgar Hoover: The Man and the Secrets*, W.W. Norton & Company, 1991, 167.

9. Jennifer Silvey, "86 Years Later, a Dark Day in Kansas City Remembered," FOX4 News, https://fox4kc.com/news/86-years-later-a-dark-day-in-kansas-city-remembered/, accessed September 2, 2021.

10. "Five Slain at Station," *Kansas City Star*, Kansas City, Missouri, June 17, 1933, 1.

11. *Ibid.*

12. *Ibid.*

13. *Ibid.*

14. *Ibid.*

15. *Ibid.*, 2.

16. Gentry, *J. Edgar Hoover: The Man and the Secrets*, 168.

17. "The FBI and the American Gangster," FBI, https://www.fbi.gov/history/brief-history/the-fbi-and-the-american-gangster, accessed August 30, 2021.

18. "Notorious Southwest Bandit Gang Falls Before Driving Force of Federal Agents," *The Reading Times*, 10.

19. Gentry, *J. Edgar Hoover: The Man and the Secrets*, 68.

20. "Crime Control Acts," Encyclopedia.com, https://www.encyclopedia.com/law/encyclopedias-almanacs-transcripts-and-maps/crime-control-acts, accessed September 3, 2021.

21. "Crime Given U.S. Warning," *The Indianapolis Star*, Indianapolis, IN, July 25, 1934, 10.

22. Marc Aronson, *Master of Deceit: J. Edgar Hoover and America in the Age of Lies*, Candlewick Press, Massachusetts, 2012, 63.

23. *Ibid.*, 62.

24. *Ibid.*

25. Gentry, *J. Edgar Hoover: The Man and the Secrets*, 169.

26. "The FBI and the American Gangster," FBI, https://www.fbi.gov/history/brief-history/the-fbi-and-the-american-gangster, accessed September 3, 2021.

27. "FBI Founded," History.com, https://www.history.com/this-day-in-history/fbi-founded, accessed September 3, 2021.

28. *Ibid.*

Chapter 12

1. "Brutal Attack on Negroes," *The San Francisco Examiner*, San Francisco, CA, February 19, 1965, 17.

2. *Ibid.*

3. Ryan M. Jones, "Who Mourns for Jimmie Lee Jackson," National Civil Rights Museum, https://www.civilrightsmuseum.org/news/posts/who-mourns-for-jimmie-lee-jackson, accessed February 16, 2021.

4. Vivienne Sanders, *Civil Rights and Social Movements in the Americas*, Hodder Education, London, UK, 2013, 58.

5. Vivienne Sanders, *Civil Rights in the USA, 1945–68*, Hodder Education, London, UK, 2008, 72.

6. *American History*, Houghton Mifflin Harcourt, Orlando, FL, 2018, 1073.

7. *Ibid.*, 1076.

8. "Jimmie Lee Jackson," Stanford: The Martin Luther King, Jr. Research and Education Institute, https://kinginstitute.stanford.edu/encyclopedia/jackson-jimmie-lee, accessed February 16, 2021.

9. Harvard Sitkoff, *The Struggle for Black Equality*, Hill and Wang, New York, NY, 2008, 174.

10. *Ibid.*, 175.

11. Ryan M. Jones, "Who Mourns for Jimmie Lee Jackson," National Civil Rights Museum, https://www.civilrightsmuseum.org/news/posts/who-mourns-for-jimmie-lee-jackson, accessed February 16, 2021.

12. "Jimmie Lee Jackson," Stanford: The Martin Luther King, Jr., Research and Education Institute, https://kinginstitute.stanford.edu/encyclopedia/jackson-jimmie-lee, accessed February 16, 2021.

13. Sitkoff, *The Struggle for Black Equality*, 176.

14. "Selma to Montgomery March," history.com, https://www.history.com/topics/black-history/selma-montgomery-march, accessed February 16, 2021.

15. Vivienne Sanders, *Civil Rights in the USA, 1945–68*, 98.

16. Joyce Appleby, *The American Vision*, McGraw Hill, Columbus, OH, 2010, 870.

17. Henretta, *America: A Concise History, Volume 2: Since 1865*, 834.

18. "Constitution of the United States," United States Senate, https://www.senate.gov/civics/constitution_item/constitution.htm, accessed February 17, 2021.

19. Henretta, *America: A Concise History, Volume 2: Since 1865*, 834.

20. "Selma to Montgomery March," Stanford: The Martin Luther King, Jr., Research and Education Institute, https://kinginstitute.stanford.edu/encyclopedia/selma-montgomery-march, accessed February 17, 2021.

21. *Ibid.*

22. *Ibid.*

23. *Ibid.*

24. Ryan M. Jones, "Who Mourns for Jimmie Lee Jackson," National Civil Rights Museum, https://www.civilrightsmuseum.org/news/posts/who-mourns-for-jimmie-lee-jackson, accessed February 17, 2021.

25. *Ibid.*

Chapter 13

1. "A Letter from Ron Ridenhour Regarding the My Lai Massacre (1969)," Alpha History, https://alphahistory.com/vietnamwar/ron-ridenhour-letter-congress-1969/, accessed February 18, 2021.

2. Davis, *Don't Know Much About History*, 486.

3. *American History*, Houghton Mifflin Harcourt, Orlando, FL, 2018, 1138.

4. *Ibid.*, 1139.

5. *Ibid.*, 1140.

6. *Ibid.*, 1144.

7. "Savage Battle Became a Walk in the Sunshine," *The Charlotte Observer*, Charlotte, NC, December 11, 1969, 18.

8. "The My Lai Massacre and Courts Martial: An Account," Famous Trials, https://famous-trials.com/mylaicourts/1656-myl-intro, accessed February 19, 2021.

9. *American History*, Houghton Mifflin Harcourt, Orlando, FL, 2018, 1152.

10. "The My Lai Massacre and Courts Martial: An Account," Famous Trials, https://famous-trials.com/mylaicourts/1656-myl-intro, accessed February 19, 2021.

11. Davis, *Don't Know Much About History*, 489.

12. *American History*, Houghton Mifflin Harcourt, Orlando, FL, 2018, 1152.

13. "Savage Battle Became a Walk in the Sunshine," *The Charlotte Observer*, Charlotte, NC, December 11, 1969, 18.

14. "The My Lai Massacre and Courts Martial: An Account," Famous Trials, https://famous-trials.com/mylaicourts/1656-myl-intro, accessed February 19, 2021.

15. "My Lai Enemy Could Have Been Woman or Child," *Fort Worth Telegram*, Fort Worth, TX, December 18, 1969, 66.

16. "My Lai: I Felt Like I Was Doing the Right Thing," *The Los Angeles Times*, Los Angeles, CA, November 30, 1969, 108.

17. *Ibid.*

18. "The My Lai Massacre and Courts Martial: An Account," Famous Trials, https://famous-trials.com/mylaicourts/1656-myl-intro, accessed February 21, 2021.

19. *Ibid.*

20. Davis, *Don't Know Much About History*, 489.

21. Leckie, *The Wars of America*, 1017–1018.

22. "The Clamor Over Calley," *Time Magazine*, April 12, 1971, Vol. 97, No. 15, 20.

23. Lilly Rothman, "Read the Letter That Changed the Way Americans Saw the Vietnam War," TIME Magazine, https://time.com/3732062/ronald-ridenhour-vietnam-my-lai/, accessed February 23, 2021.

24. Appleby, *The American Vision*, 899.

25. James S. Olson and Randy Roberts, *Where the Domino Fell: America and Vietnam, 1945 to 1990*, St. Martin's Press, New York, NY, 1991, 229.

26. *Ibid.*

27. *American History*, Houghton Mifflin Harcourt, Orlando, FL, 2018, 1152.

Epilogue

1. Josiah Bates, "2020 Will End as One of America's Most Violent Years in Decades," TIME Magazine, https://time.com/5922082/2020-gun-violence-homicides-record-year/, accessed February 24, 2021.

2. *Ibid.*

Bibliography

Anderson, Fred. *Crucible of War: The Seven Years' War and the Fate of Empire in British North America, 1754–1766.* Vintage Books, 2001.

Anderson, Fred. *The War That Made America: A Short History of the French and Indian War.* Penguin Books, 2006.

Aronson, Marc. *Master of Deceit: J. Edgar Hoover and America in the Age of Lies.* Candlewick Press, 2019.

Bailey, Thomas Andrew. *A Diplomatic History of the American People.* 1942.

Beezley, William H., and Michael C. Meyer, eds. *The Oxford History of Mexico.* Oxford University Press, 2010.

Beringer, Richard E. *Why the South Lost the Civil War.* University of Georgia Press, 2000.

Billington, Ray Allen. *American History After 1865.* Littlefield, Adams & Co., 1953.

Borneman, Walter R. *The French and Indian War: Deciding the Fate of North America.* Harper Perennial, 2007.

Brown, Dee. *Bury My Heart at Wounded Knee: An Indian History of the American West.* Fall River Press, 2014.

Calloway, Colin G. *The Indian World of George Washington: The First President, the First Americans, and the Birth of the Nation.* Oxford University Press, 2019.

Chernow, Ron. *Washington: A Life.* Penguin, 2010.

Cooper, John Milton, Jr. *Pivotal Decades: The United States, 1900–1920.* Norton, 1990.

Cozzens, Peter. *Tecumseh and the Prophet: The Shawnee Brothers Who Defied a Nation.* Alfred A. Knopf, 2020.

Cummins, D. Duane, and William Gee White. *Contrasting Decades: The 1920s and 1930s.* Benziger, 1979.

Cunliffe, Marcus. *The Nation Takes Shape: 1789–1837.* University of Chicago Press, 1980.

David, Henry. *The History of the Haymarket Affair: A Study of the American Social-Revolutionary and Labor Movements.* Collier Books, 1963.

Davidson, James West, and Mark H. Lytle. *After the Fact: The Art of Historical Detection.* McGraw-Hill, 2010.

Davis, Kenneth C. *Don't Know Much About History: Everything You Need to Know About History but Never Learned.* Harper, 2011.

Dickson, Paul, and Thomas B. Allen. *The Bonus Army: An American Epic.* Dover Publications, 2020.

Donald, David, ed. *Why the North Won the Civil War.* Collier Books, Macmillan Publishing Company, 1993.

Eisenhower, John S. D. *Intervention!: The United States and the Mexican Revolution, 1913–1917.* W.W. Norton, 1995.

Bibliography

Ferling, John E. *A Leap in the Dark: The Struggle to Create the American Republic.* Oxford University Press, 2003.

Fiffer, Steve, and Adar Cohen. *Jimmie Lee & James: Two Lives, Two Deaths, and the Movement That Changed America.* Regan Arts, 2015.

Foner, Eric. *Give Me Liberty! An American History.* W.W. Norton, 2011.

Foote, Shelby. *The Civil War: A Narrative.* Vintage Books, 1986.

Gentry, Curt. *J. Edgar Hoover: The Man and the Secrets.* Norton, 2001.

Grandin, Greg. *Empire's Workshop: Latin America, the United States, and the Rise of the New Imperialism.* Henry Holt and Company, 2010.

Guinn, Jeff. *War on the Border: Villa, Pershing, the Texas Rangers, and an American Invasion.* Simon & Schuster, 2021.

Gwynne, S. C. *Rebel Yell: The Violence, Passion, and Redemption of Stonewall Jackson.* Scribner's, an Imprint of Simon & Schuster, 2015.

Hofstadter, Richard. *American Political Tradition and the Men Who Made It.* Vintage Books, 1989.

Johnson, Paul. *George Washington: The Founding Father.* Harper Perennial, 2009.

Johnson, Paul E. *The Early American Republic: 1789–1829.* Oxford University Press, 2007.

Karnow, Stanley. *Vietnam: A History.* Viking, 1991.

Klotter, James C. *History Mysteries.* University Press of Kentucky, 2011.

LaFeber, Walter. *Inevitable Revolutions: The United States in Central America.* W.W. Norton, 1993.

LaFeber, Walter, Richard Polenberg, and Nancy Woloch. *The American Century: A History of the United States Since the 1890s.* M.E. Sharpe, 2013.

Leckie, Robert. *The Wars of America.* Harper Perennial, 1993.Long, David F. *The Outward View: An Illustrated History of United States Foreign Relations.* Rand McNally, 1964.

Loomis, Erik. *A History of America in Ten Strikes.* New Press, 2020.

Meacham, Jon. *American Lion: Andrew Jackson in the White House.* Random House, 2009.

Millett, Allan R. *For the Common Defense: A Military History of the United States of America.* Free Press, 1994.

Muzzey, David Saville. *A History of Our Country: A Textbook for High-school Students.* Ginn and Company, 1943.

Nicolay, John G., and John Hay, eds. *Complete Works of Abraham Lincoln.* 1894.

Olson, James Stuart, and Randy Roberts. *Where the Domino Fell: America and Vietnam, 1945 to 1990.* St. Martin's Press, 1996.

Owens, Robert M. *Mr. Jefferson's Hammer: William Henry Harrison and the Origins of American Indian Policy.* University of Oklahoma Press, 2011.

Parsons, Lynn H. *The Birth of Modern Politics: Andrew Jackson, John Quincy Adams, and the Election of 1828.* Oxford University Press, 2011.

Potter, David Morris, and Don Edward Fehrenbacher. *The Impending Crisis: America Before the Civil War: 1848–1861.* Harper Perennial, 2011.

Reynolds, David S. *John Brown, Abolitionist: The Man Who Killed Slavery, Sparked the Civil War, and Seeded Civil Rights.* Vintage Books, 2005.

Richardson, Heather Cox. *Wounded Knee: Party Politics and the Road to an American Massacre.* ReadHowYouWant, 2011.

Rubin, Richard. *The Last of the Doughboys: The Forgotten Generation and Their Forgotten World War.* Houghton Mifflin Harcourt, 2014.

Rulli, Joseph Anthony. *The Chicago Haymarket Affair: A Guide to a Labor Rights Milestone.* History Press, 2016.

Bibliography

Russell, Francis. *Sacco & Vanzetti: The Case Resolved*. Harper & Row, 1986.

Sanders, Vivienne. *Civil Rights and Social Movements in the Americas*. Hodder Education, 2013.

Sitkoff, Harvard. *The Struggle for Black Equality*. Hill and Wang, 2008.

Sugden, John. *Tecumseh: A Life*. Paw Prints, 2008.

Sugden, John. *Tecumseh's Last Stand*. University of Oklahoma Press, 1989.

Temkin, Moshik. *The Sacco-Vanzetti Affair: America on Trial*. Yale University Press, 2011.

Topp, Michael Miller. *The Sacco and Vanzetti Case: A Brief History with Documents*. Palgrave Macmillan, 2005.

Velie, Alan R. *American Indian Literature: An Anthology*. University of Oklahoma Press, 1991.

Waters, W. W., and William Carter White. *B.E.F.: The Whole Story of the Bonus Army*. Cincinnatus Press, 2007.

Weiner, Tim. *Enemies: A History of the FBI*. Random House Trade Paperbacks, 2013.

Whyte, Kenneth. *Hoover: An Extraordinary Life in Extraordinary Times*. Vintage Books, 2018.

Zinn, Howard. *A People's History of the United States: 1492–Present*. Routledge, Taylor & Francis Group, 2015.

Index

Index

Index

Index

Index

Index